Last Minute

Interview

Tips

By
Brandon Toropov

CAREER PRESS
3 Tice Road
P.O. Box 687
Franklin Lakes, NJ 07417
1-800-CAREER-1
201-848-0310 (NJ and outside U.S.)
FAX: 201-848-1727

LAST MINUTE INTERVIEW TIPS
ISBN 1-56414-240-X, $7.99
Cover design by Foster & Foster
Printed in the U.S.A. by Book-mart Press

To order this title by mail, please include price as noted above, $2.50 handling per order, and $1.00 for each book ordered. Send to: Career Press, Inc., 3 Tice Road, P.O. Box 687, Franklin Lakes, NJ 07417.

Or call toll-free 1-800-CAREER-1 (NJ and Canada: 201-848-0310) to order using VISA or MasterCard, or for further information on books from Career Press.

Library of Congress Cataloging-in-Publication Data

Toropov, Brandon.
    Last minute interview tips / By Brandon Toropov.
        p.   cm.
    Includes index.
    ISBN 1-56414-240-X (pbk.)
    1. Employment interviewing--United States. 2. Job hunting--United States.   I. Title.
HF5549.5.I6T67   1996
650.14--dc20   96-13886
                                                            CIP

To

David, Stephen and Julia

Acknowledgments

Without Ron Fry, this book would never have come into existence.

Glenn KnicKrehm, Leslie Tragert and Robert Tragert all offered support and help to me during the time it was being written.

Paul McCartney, George Harrison, Ringo Starr and Yoko Ono were nice enough to release *The Beatles Anthology,* which served as essential musical background while I was writing. (Author's note: If you play Beatles music during the breaks in your job search when you're unwinding from your research and contact work, you'll get better job offers!)

Contents

Introduction

You have to get ready for a job interview. Fast.

How can you find out what you need to know about the company, given the amount of time that you have available? What interview questions should you prepare for? What will you do if they throw a stress question your way—and how will you know the purpose underlying that kind of question? Most important of all, *what should you do first?*

The book you're holding in your hands will outline a detailed program that will help you develop the best possible interview strategy given the time you have available. It will help you prioritize your research, prepare for the toughest questions you're likely to face, and give you solid advice on dealing with the curve balls you can expect the interviewer to toss your way.

In addition to supplying you with practical, detailed battle plans and sample responses to the most commonly asked questions, this book will also offer important insights on how to follow up appropriately *after* your interview...an important step your competitors will, in all likelihood, overlook or minimize. (See Appendix 1 for details on this crucial part of your job search campaign.)

By following the advice in this book, you can make the upcoming interview time *your prime time*, your time to shine...even if you only have one day to prepare!

Your attitude toward the interview process is all-important—far more important than the amount of time you have available now to get ready. In fact, if I had to boil the guiding idea behind this book down into a single sentence, it would probably read something like this:

> *People like to hire those who show persistent optimism.*

Typically, an author wishes his readers "good luck" at this point of the book. That's not necessary in the present situation. The nice thing about the program that you've hooked up with is that it *removes the need for luck* and puts you in control of the interview process, no matter how much time you have to prepare for it. For my part, I've come to the conclusion that luck doesn't really exist in human affairs. Other things *do* exist, things that are frequently *mistaken* for luck: preparation, a persistently positive attitude and the willingness to develop and seize opportunities.

Enough talking. You have an interview to prepare for. As you set out to put this system into action, I wish you all you really need for success on the job front—and, for that matter, in the business world in general: A willingness to see the positive implications of unexpected events, and a battle plan to go back to, or revise, as circumstances dictate. If you've got those two assets, you're not going to need luck—you'll make it for yourself.

—B.T.

Chapter 1

You

Let's get right to the point. The best way to impress an interviewer is to relay personal success stories that illustrate positive aspects of your career, and to deliver these in an upbeat, optimistic manner. Preparing such stories can serve you well in all manner of situations, but these anecdotes are particularly important to have at the tip of your tongue when time to prepare for an interview is short.

Even if you have only one day to prepare yourself for an interview, your first task should be to prepare personal success stories along the lines suggested in this chapter.

The big advantage to personal success stories? They help you overcome the toughest questions!

In difficult interview situations, you will find yourself in a position to follow the lead of some of our finest politicians—*if* you have prepared a story that illustrates one of your strong suits. Just as a shrewd political figure who has been tossed a tough question must find a way to respond with something other than, "Well, gee, that's a tough one, and I hadn't really given it much thought," so must you.

The formula for responding to an impossible question (such as "How do you respond to allegations that you asked a zebra out on a date in 1986?") is pretty straightforward:

- Acknowledge and restate the question. ("I'm glad you asked me about that zebra matter, because it gives me the opportunity to address some pressing zoo-related questions. People have a right to know about such important issues.")

- Initiate a smooth transition. Hook the question up with the prepared answer at your disposal that comes closest to dealing with the question posed. ("Although I can't recall any discussion along the lines you mention, I think it is important to point out that, as Mayor of Middleton, I increased funding for zoo improvements by 43 percent over a two-year period without raising taxes,...")

- Conclude by addressing a specific point of the questioner's in a forward-looking way. ("And in addition, my administration restored the ostrich display to its past glory. Now, there may be other issues that need to be addressed and resolved with regard to my personal contacts with individual inhabitants of the Middleton Zoo, and I'd be more than willing to review the records on that score for you if that turns out to be a step we need to take. But the point I want to make now is, we must maintain appropriate, legal and attractive housing for all members of the animal kingdom, both in my home town and in the state at large.")

Does this mean you should make a practice of dodging questions?

No! The idea is to find some way to turn the question, as posed, toward one of your strong suits. Sometimes, when politicians try this, it looks like a bit of a stretch—as in the example here—but the technique may also allow them to demonstrate poise under fire and an ability to look to the long-term in an optimistic way. And anyway, it certainly beats shrugging one's shoulders or pleading the Fifth Amendment, right?

In order to make this "ultimate fall-back" work for you, however, you must do some research on yourself. Yes, you read right—knowing the specifics of your own strengths and weaknesses must come before you research the prospective employer. That research is essential, of course: You shouldn't walk into any interview without <u>having some idea of the products and services the company offers, the competition it faces and the strategic problems it must overcome</u>. But the bedrock of your interview is *you,* and that's the commodity we're going to focus on first.

Many job seekers make the mistake of saying (and thinking) something along the following lines:

- "I don't have a job right now."
- "I'm looking for work."
- "Somebody needs to hire me as a..."
- "I'm unemployed."
- "I don't really like my job. What I *want* to be is a..."
- "I'm looking for a job as a..."

These innocent-sounding sentiments, whether spoken or repeated silently, may put your job search effort on a fatally flawed foundation! The fact is, you *do* have a job, right now. Whether it feels like it or not, you are in marketing and sales. And your product is you.

Because you are trying to find the best possible market for a very important product—yourself—you owe it to yourself to do a little bit of initial research about that product. When you're done with that research, you must attend to the demands of your marketing job (in particular, preparing for an imminent job interview) with the same diligence, professionalism, competence, thoroughness and enthusiasm you would show in any other workplace situation. After all, if you don't show the prospective employer such qualities during the time you spend on *this* job, the one that features *you,* how can you expect him or her to trust you with the important responsibilities of any *other* position?

Your job search campaign in general, and your interview in particular, will serve as a demonstration to the employer of your ability to deal with the same tough situations you may face on the job.

Preparing intelligently crafted success stories from your own background will help you demonstrate how seriously you take the interview—and that, in turn, will demonstrate how seriously you are likely to take the job you are after. Although the specific facts you present in the interview will certainly matter a great deal, the *way* you pass along your success stories may carry just as much weight with your interviewer.

In this part of the book, you'll learn about some important advice on developing and delivering the success stories that will help you come out ahead during the interview and land the job offer you deserve.

Keeping up with the times

News flash! Lifelong careers with one benevolent, paternalistic employer have pretty much gone the way of the buggy-whip. Why? Well, for one thing, *today's companies have to react more quickly and effectively than ever before* to the challenges they face in the marketplace. As crazy as the *employment* world may look to you right now, you may rest assured that the world of business looks even more unpredictable to the people who are trying to build profitable companies.

We live in a world in which "international companies" can emerge, grow or fail overnight, thanks to a snazzy home page on the World Wide Web. We live in a world in which demand for once-essential products and services can be superseded in an instant as a result of new technological developments.

What does that mean? It means that, for the prospective employer, and for you, *adaptability is everything.*

In today's economy, a work force made up of people who can each perform a single set of tasks quite well can be a serious handicap. If each worker's focus is on a narrowly written job description, the company may not be able to react as quickly to competitive challenges. Today's workers want employees who can spot problems, train themselves more or less independently to resolve them, and pass the information along to colleagues as circumstances require.

These days, prospective employers don't want to hear about formal job titles as much as they want to know about the inventive ways you've dealt with the problems that *no one foresaw*.

Accordingly, you must find success stories from your personal history that show your willingness, ability, and, yes, your *eagerness* to work outside the formal confines of your title. "That's not my department" is an obscenity on the employment front these days, so don't say it.

You should assume that the person you'll be interviewing with will be on the lookout for workers who show the ability to adapt well to *brand-new* ideas and procedures. They *want* to talk to people who can show a little initiative when circumstances dictate, which is most of the time. So you're going to pass along stories that demonstrate that you are this kind of person.

> *The success stories you develop for your interview must show your ability to* **adapt well to new ideas and procedures.** *They must demonstrate that you are not wedded to the narrow confines of a written job description.*

Warning: Demonstrating your flexibility is *not* the same thing as saying that you are "willing to do anything"! That's a message that puts the responsibility on the employer, not on you. What we're talking about is sending a message of accountable flexibility.

Your aim is to demonstrate a specific set of skills in a certain area...and a willingness to adapt those skills *to other, unexpected problems* as they arise. It's time to work up *compelling success stories* from your past that highlight this trait. Do so right now.

Take a few moments to jot down the details of five separate occasions in your work, educational or volunteer history when you adapted well to a new setting.

If you're like most of us, the first few minutes will be the toughest, but after that, you'll probably find that you can come up with a great many more than five examples!

Take this opportunity to think of the times you mastered new computer software, pitched in when a supervisor was ill or performed well when given a new set of responsibilities in an area in which you had little or no experience. Use nonwork-related examples if, after 10 or 15 minutes, you are still having trouble identifying work stories.

Here are some examples of what your stories might sound like. Be sure to incorporate *your own* experiences, not to simply adapt what follows to your own situation. Don't exaggerate—*do* make the most of the positive, can-do adaptability stories in your own background.

Sample success stories: adaptability to new systems and ideas

"We were launching a new product, and the director of marketing wanted to ship out some free samples to 2,000 important retailers. The problem was that this person's assistant, who would normally have handled the data entry portion of the job, was out with the flu, and the samples had to arrive before a major national television promotion that couldn't be rescheduled.

"I volunteered to stay late three nights that week and do the entry work on the director's computer system— even though I was technically part of the accounting department. Well, it worked out quite well—the mailing of free samples went out right on time, and the director made a point of submitting a written thank-you note for inclusion in my salary review that year. I think that might have had something to do with the nice raise I got, to tell you the truth."

∽ ∽ ∽ ∽ ∽

"One week, the operations manager was sick, and I was put in charge of the department by default. There was an unexpected delivery from a shipper that no one had told me about. I really wasn't sure what I was supposed to do and couldn't reach anyone on the phone. There was no room in the warehouse to store the merchandise, but I knew that what was coming in was something the president of the company had been talking about at a big meeting with my boss.

"I authorized a rental of warehouse space so we didn't have to refuse the shipment and send it back to the manufacturer. It was a lucky thing I did—the manufacturer was located in Seoul, Korea!"

Keep your eye on the bottom line

During the interview, you're also going to use success stories to pass along the second key message: *your profit orientation and productivity.*

The watchword in today's economy is efficiency. Employees who live simply to "punch the clock" shouldn't expect much in the way of career success or stability. To win the job offer you truly deserve, you must convey your desire to accomplish a little bit more than keeping up with office gossip, submitting your picks to the office football pool and filling out expense reports once a month.

Odds are, the person who will be interviewing you wants to talk to someone who won't require any convincing that the reason to show up for work in the first place is to help the organization attain its primary goals.

> *The success stories you develop for your interview must show your ability to **help the organization operate efficiently.** You must provide compelling anecdotes that show you are determined to deliver the profits and/or results the prospective employer must commit to.*

It's time to develop several *quantifiable* examples illustrating how your on-the-job ideas paid off, or how you've resolved (or helped to resolve) dilemmas in the workplace. What have you done that led to savings or increased revenue for the organization you worked for? Use specific figures to cite improved performance in a particular area.

The stories you develop in this category are of paramount importance in your interview preparation work. Take some time now—at least 20 to 30 minutes, and perhaps as much as 90 minutes—to develop as many examples of your efficiency and profit orientation as possible.

Bear in mind that you'll strengthen your case if you can appeal to independent sources: quotes from your own salary reviews, annual company reports, sales reports, amounts on commission checks and so on. Make every effort to use *actual figures* to bolster your success stories. If you must give estimates, be sure they're responsible, and note that they are estimates.

The process may be difficult at first, but stay with it. Ask yourself questions like these:

- What was the last crisis or emergency situation that you helped to resolve? What would have happened if you had done nothing?
- How much would it cost your employer if you simply refused, for a whole day, to do any of the things you normally do on the job?
- Were you ever responsible for taking over a project or initiative someone else did not seem capable of completing satisfactorily? What would have happened if that person had simply continued working on the job in the same ineffective way?

These stories may represent the most important part of your interview preparation work. Don't short-change yourself. Take the time to develop compelling anecdotes.

Sample success stories: efficiency and profit orientation

"On my January performance review, I was cited as, quoting here, 'a positive, upbeat force who's a real plus for the entire department.' My supervisor recommended a 14-percent raise, the highest he was allowed to submit. I think the main reason for that choice was my work on the Vocabulab project, which I more or less developed from scratch, and which sold 35,000 units during its first year of release."

"My overtime work on the Peterson project allowed us to submit our bid two days earlier than we would otherwise have done. If I hadn't put that time in, we would have missed the deadline—and lost a $200,000 project."

"By setting up a car pool and phone tree in my department, I was able to reduce weather-related absenteeism by 25 percent, compared to the same period of the previous year. My boss told me that he thought I'd saved the company at least two person-weeks in lost productivity over the course of the year."

Present yourself with a marketing orientation

People who have a solid market orientation are quite comfortable talking to their organization's customers and prospective customers, even though they may not hold jobs that relate directly to sales or marketing. You must use stories from your past to show the interviewer that you have a sense of what the product or service in question does, who it does that for and what advantages the target company holds over its competitors.

The success stories you develop for your interview must demonstrate your **market orientation and product/service knowledge,** *even if you are not applying for a sales or marketing position.*

A working knowledge of the target company's products and services, as well as an understanding of its customer base, is essential in today's employment market. You'll find ideas on how to track down this knowledge, as it relates to your target employer, later on in this book. Eventually, you should be able to discuss, at the drop of a hat, new ways the company might market its products and services.

For now, think of situations where you had to develop a "sales mind-set" in a past or present position. Cite examples in which you dealt well with customers and prospective customers. Here are three examples.

Sample success stories: market orientation and sales/product knowledge

"As part of a research project I was working on for my boss, I had to interview potential customers for a new product the company was considering launching. The feedback I passed along from the people I spoke with turned out to be essential to the success of the product. And the interviews I conducted helped to identify some potentially serious design flaws."

"Once, at my previous job, there was a scheduling error and there were no front-desk people to man the phones for customer queries over the toll-free line. This happened during the middle of a major national advertising campaign! I volunteered to help out, and it was a very positive experience all the way around. I had to learn on my feet, and the first few calls I had to ask for a little help from people. But I soon got the hang of it. Fortunately, I was already familiar with the promotion and the product line."

"After graduating from college, I worked as a telemarketer for a telecommunications firm. I did cold calls for a line of pocket pagers, and I sold quite a few of them. I didn't stay in the job for long, because I found a job in a publishing setting that made more sense for me. But I did make Salesperson of the Month twice during my time there. I was proud of that."

Important note: In today's employment environment, displaying market orientation to the prospective employer

is vitally important, even *(especially)* if your career experience and career objectives do not relate to marketing or
sales. In addition to brief stories of the kind outlined here,
you should develop at least one extended story that shows
your market orientation to the greatest advantage.

The anecdote should show how you overcame significant obstacles to post *respectable* (not necessarily spectacu-
lar) results when called upon to deal with customers or potential customers. Here's an example:

*"I can't claim to have much of a sales background,
and I've never worked as a salesperson officially, as
far as job descriptions go. But I did have a fascinating
experience along these lines that may be worth
discussing. I once had to fill in when three of my
company's top people came down with the flu right
before an extremely important trade show.*

*"As a general rule this event represented something
like 30 percent of the company's annual business, so
people were a little worried when the president, the
vice president of marketing and the vice president of
marketing's assistant all got so sick that they couldn't
make the trip. The job of manning the booth and
asking for orders fell to me and to the president's
personal assistant—and neither of us had ever
attended this trade show before!*

*"We got a telephone briefing from the president and a
brief set of written instructions from the vice president
of marketing. And that was it. We had one day to
prepare, and we spent most of it memorizing names
from the company address book, names of people we
were likely to meet. At the end of the day, the office
manager handed us a couple of airline tickets and
wished us luck. We did some role-playing exercises on
the plane, and we kept it up that night at the hotel.*

"The first day of the show, the assistant and I showed up at 7 a.m., set up the exhibit, then took turns dashing to the restroom so we could change out of our work clothes and into our business suits! Well, we did $262,000 of business over the three days of the show—which was about 90 percent of the amount the event usually generated. We thought that was pretty good for a couple of rookies."

Your objective is not necessarily to demonstrate that you achieved superior sales results (unless you're looking for a job as a salesperson). Rather, the in-depth story you develop should outline a time when you had to deal directly with the people who actually used and/or bought the product or service your company provided. And it should show, in a compelling fashion, exactly how you kept them happy.

೧ ೧ ೧ ೧ ೧

To summarize, then, you will want to use the ideas that follow in this book to demonstrate specifically that:

- You are adaptable and deal well with change.
- You know that efficiency and bottom-line results are essential.
- You have a good sense of the organization's products and/or services, and you can explain what the company has to offer in a compelling way to a prospective customer.

"Hey, wait a minute!"

Do you feel a little funny about highlighting these aspects of your employment background? That's a natural reaction. As you look over the list of stories you're supposed to develop, you may find yourself wondering, "Aren't the things I'm offering to provide to the employer—the ability to manage change well, the ability to deliver results efficiently and profitably and a sense of marketing flair—aren't those the very same problems my *superiors* are supposed to be keeping an eye out for?"

Today's economic and business realities demand that you become, to a certain extent, *your own manager*. That's the often-overlooked implication of all the downsizing and short-staffing in our economy. When employers *do* decide to take on new people, they do so because they think the hires have a good chance of working well *on their own*.

You're not done yet

You should eventually memorize the details of your success stories and be prepared to recite them at a moment's notice. However, you will need much more information than these stories. During the interview, you must be able to demonstrate that the specifics of your job history match up with the requirements of the employer. That means developing a detailed written file reflecting your job history.

Prepare a separate sheet for every full-time and part-time job you've held, no matter how short the tenure. (See my companion book, *Last Minute Job Search Tips*, for sample forms.) Yes, even summer jobs are important here. They demonstrate resourcefulness, responsibility and initiative.

Employment

For each employer, include:

- Name, address and telephone number.
- The names of all your supervisors and, whenever possible, where they can be reached.
- Letter of recommendation, if they cannot be reached.
- The exact dates (month/year) you were employed.

For each job, include:

- Your specific duties and responsibilities.
- Supervisory experience, noting the number of people you supervised.
- Specific skills required for the job.
- Your key accomplishments.
- The dates you received promotions.
- Awards, honors and special recognition received.

For each part-time job, include:

- The number of hours you worked per week.

Volunteer work

Make a detailed record of your volunteer pursuits, similar to the one you've just completed for each job you've held.

For each volunteer organization, include:

- Name, address and telephone number.
- The name and address of your supervisor or the director of the organization.
- Letter of recommendation.
- The exact dates (month/year) of your involvement with the organization.

For each volunteer experience, include:

- The approximate number of hours you devoted to the activity each month.
- Your specific duties and responsibilities.
- Specific skills required.
- Accomplishments.
- Awards, honors and special recognition received.

Awards and honors

List all the awards and honors you've received from schools, community groups, church groups, clubs and so on. You may include awards from prestigious high schools (prep schools or professional schools) even if you're in graduate school or long out of college.

Other

You should also list any appropriate information reflecting hobbies, extracurricular activities, military service and foreign language ability.

"Hmm...did I overlook something?"

Now you'll probably find yourself thinking about revisions you could make to the success stories you developed a little earlier. Not to worry—that's exactly what you *should* to be thinking! Are there other incidents that do a better job of demonstrating your ability to deal well with change, your profit orientation and your ability to assume a sales/marketing mind-set? Can you think of a better way to present a particular story?

Even if your time is extremely tight, your performance during the interview is worth preparing for properly. Your ability to project a positive, confident persona while delivering a powerful success story tells the employer some very important things about you. You are polite, but persistent; you know how to take charge; you handle potentially stressful situations well.

Take a few minutes now to review your success stories closely and make all appropriate revisions. Once you do, you'll be ready to move on to the next chapter.

Chapter 2

The employer

If your time is extremely tight, you won't have a whole lot of time to research the prospective employer. As you'll see, though, even a single day is enough to find out *something* of value about the prospective employer.

Even if you haven't done any meaningful research on the company yet, you can rest assured that there is one company-related topic your interviewer will be very interested in hearing about: Your level of commitment to the job, company and industry in question.

"I know what I want!"

The advice that follows in this book assumes that you know—roughly—about the type of work you want to do in the industry within which you'll be interviewing. A *firm sense of purpose* on this point may just be your most important asset when dealing with the interviewer.

Employers can tell when you're in the game for the love *and* the money, and they know that people who fit this description generally make the best (and happiest) employees. Yet the sad fact remains that, in the work force today, employers simply don't give guarantees. Your aim is to secure a job offer as a result of your interview—not to get the employer to take care of you for the rest of your life. You should, accordingly, demonstrate a strong, sense of confidence and autonomy to go along with your commitment to deliver results in your chosen field.

> *During the interview, you must let the prospective employer know that you have decided without regret or hesitation to focus on* this *job, with* this *company, in* this *industry. You must show you have a clear idea of exactly what you want to get accomplished, and that you are itching to start. Most employers can sense this passion. It is an extremely attractive trait, one that interviewers almost universally respond to in a positive way.*

It's worth noting here that your chosen industry *does not* have to be the one in which you've spent time previously. You can use success stories to demonstrate the specific ways your talents can *translate* to concerns common to hiring managers in virtually *all* industries.

Why go to the trouble of focusing closely on your commitment to the target company's industry? Because hiring someone is a pretty big deal these days. It's more expensive than ever, as is training the person hired. Many employees turn out to represent serious legal problems to the officials who hired them (and regretted doing so). And you probably don't need this book to remind you that margins are tight; that competition, both foreign and domestic, is brutal; that technology is advancing at a dizzying pace.

If it will help a company's margin to pass over an applicant who seems a little less committed to long-term success in the industry, a little less self-directed, a little less amenable to change, a little more likely to make trouble or throw up his or her hands when things go wrong, then guess what? The company will take a pass on that person's candidacy.

> *The "I'm committed to this industry for the long-term" attitude during your interviews will serve instant notice that you represent the kind of employee people need—today.*

The 10 commandments for demonstrating commitment

First Commandment: Thou Shalt Not Share Thy Ambivalence with the Interviewer. If you harbor doubts about the wisdom of working with this company, keep them to yourself. (You may be able to parlay an offer from this firm into action on the part of one of your other target companies.)

Second Commandment: Thou Shalt State Clearly Thy Desire to Work for This Particular Company. Displaying a sense of certainty on this point, and backing it up with the research you've done to determine a good "fit," is a great way to win the interviewer's interest and attention. If you're engaged in multiple interviews with various firms, you will need to choose your words carefully, but the message should still be "I'm talking to you because I know I can make a contribution here, and I'm eager to find a way to do so."

Third Commandment: Thou Shalt Make Thyself Aware of the Most Recent Major Developments within the Target Company's Industry. If you haven't been reading the trade journals and magazines associated with the industry, you should take the time to do this before the interview.

Fourth Commandment: Thou Shalt Learn What the Company Does Before Walking in the Door for the Interview. Even if you are short on time, you must make some attempt to find out about the prospective employer's operations. Most of your competitors won't bother to do much research. Don't be like them. See the later chapters of this book for detailed advice on how to get the most research done in the least amount of time.

Fifth Commandment: Thou Shalt Let the Employer Know That Thou Enjoyest the Various Challenges of the Industry. Did you ever wonder about the best unspoken in-person message you can send, the one most likely to land you a job offer? It's pretty simple. *Enjoy yourself, even when others wouldn't.* Most of us like to run into individuals for whom life is a joy, not a chore. People who adopt and *keep* an optimistic mind-set during the job search are much likelier to secure the cooperation, advice, and help of decision-makers. Make it clear that you are focusing on this industry and this company because you *like* the work associated with them.

Sixth Commandment: Thou Shalt Never Come Across as Desperate. Let's pretend you're a manager with hiring authority. Which of these two personality types would *you* be more likely to want hanging around the office eight hours a day?

> *"Mr. Smith, I'm going to level with you. Things are tight at our household. If I can't start work with your company next week, I don't know what I'm going to do. I'll take anything. Anything at all. But I've simply got to get a job, and if I don't get one with you, I'm not sure what's going to happen to my family."*

"Mr. Smith, I've got some ideas about how you can dramatically increase productivity in your division. The strategies I'm talking about helped me post a 20-percent boost in output when I was a manager at General Widget. I'd like to implement these ideas for your company on a full-time basis."

There's no contest, right? Unless you have an affinity for listening to whining, you'd probably *much* rather talk to the second person than the first. So would the interviewer. *Depression and desperation don't sell, but poise and confidence do.* Remember that single-minded pursuit of the goal of finding the right job within your chosen industry is not the same thing as *begging and pleading* for that job.

Seventh Commandment: Thou Shalt Focus on Functions, Not Job Titles. This is especially important to remember if you are trying to enter a brand-new field. Emphasize what you did, rather than what you were called while you were doing it. Emphasize the tangible ways you benefited your employer, rather than the technical terminology your employer used to describe what you were up to. If you focus too much on words and phrases that are not familiar to your interviewer, he or she may conclude— erroneously—that there's no match.

Eighth Commandment: Thou Shalt Demonstrate Computer Literacy Relevant to the Industry. If there's a perceived experience gap arising from your lack of work in this industry, you will need to make it clear that you can make sense of the big job—tackling this company's computer system—by appealing to your success on other systems. Highlight as many similarities as you can between those systems and the one you would face as part of this job. (And if, as the 21st century dawns, you cannot be troubled even to master a word processing or spreadsheet program, you should not be surprised if your job search is a long and frustrating one.)

Ninth Commandment: Thou Shalt Not Pretend to Know What Thou Dost Not. Shifting the subject to something you *do* know is perfectly acceptable. Attempting to fake your way through a technical inquiry or lie about your experience base is a big mistake—one that will only convince the interviewer that your desire to work within the industry is ill-founded.

Tenth Commandment: Thou Shalt Embrace Change. This is the only constant in the business environment most decision-makers face. If you're in doubt as to the best ways to project your willingness to deal well with potentially chaotic situations, review the adaptability success stories you developed in Chapter 1.

Congratulations!

If you've read this much of the book carefully and followed all the specific advice you've received up to this point, you're ready to move on to the next phase of the book.

What, exactly, should you do to prepare for that interview that's coming up? You'll find the answers in the pages that follow.

Chapter 3

If you have an interview *tomorrow*

Can you really expect to get anything accomplished with only 24 hours to prepare for a job interview? Sure. In this chapter, you'll find a list of simple steps you can take that will help you beat the clock and win the job.

Important note! This chapter assumes that because you have 24 hours to prepare for an interview, you've found some way to clear the decks and devote the research and preparation time you need for at least one full working day. If that means taking a personal day, you should find a way to do that. If that means finding someone else to take care of your children while you attend to the job of getting a job, you should find a way to do that. *If the interview is worth going to, it is worth preparing for!*

First, review your success stories

Remember, these aren't just *any* stories illustrating success in a work, volunteer or academic setting, but carefully selected incidents from your past that illustrate your:

- Ability to adapt to new systems, procedures, technologies and organizational structures.
- Market orientation—your ability to come up with new ideas for products and services, and deal effectively with customers and prospective customers.

- Bottom-line orientation—your understanding of the value of efficiency, and the notion that private organizations exist to make a profit.

If you've prepared stories that illustrate these three points, and you can deliver them confidently at a moment's notice, you've got half the battle won already.

As you get started in earnest, think of the next 24 hours as an exciting time, not as the trial of the century. Sure, time is tight, but that's kind of fun—if you look at things from a certain angle. One of the biggest mistakes you can make is to overprepare for an interview, or to look at it as an ordeal comparable to the Spanish Inquisition.

Even in interviews that *are* designed to be ordeals—stress interviews, in which the prospective employer is hoping to duplicate the conditions of an extremely difficult job setting— the best advice is to stay cool and not give the impression that you're taking things so seriously that you're likely to overlook important steps in dealing with problems.

If you spend the next 24 hours gulping coffee and memorizing materials far into the night, you won't come across as the serene, focused candidate the employer wants to hire. You're more likely to remind the interviewer of Martin Short's caricature of the hyperanxious, chain-smoking corporate executive under the gun in a *60 Minutes*-like exposé: "I knew that! I think it's so funny that you would think that I didn't know that! Of course I knew that!"

It's great to learn everything you can about the company or the problems you'd be likely to face on the job, but confidence and poise count for something, too. Don't stress out or attempt to "cram" for the interview.

You have something to offer the prospective employer; he or she has something to offer you. You're going to meet to talk about things. The worst thing that can happen? This company won't offer you a job *now*. You'll certainly be able to try again later if you want to.

The employer needs to be able to see who you are and how you handle problems. Your basic qualities are going to stay the same between now and tomorrow, so don't try to reinvent yourself. Relax and have a little fun.

You are, after all, the star of the show. This is a fascinating, exhilarating period, not an arraignment. You've got the opportunity to demonstrate your best side to someone, and the name of the game is keeping the machinery running smoothly so you can do just that. If you think of the day's work as an adventure, rather than a tribunal, you'll be that much better prepared to dazzle 'em during the interview.

Three hours for company research

Assuming you've prepared your success stories as outlined in Chapter 1, your best bet is to take *three hours and three hours only* to try to develop (or add to) your intelligence file on the company at which you'll be interviewing. If you have to work on your success stories today, do that first and reduce later time allotments accordingly.

Here, in descending order of importance, is a list of tasks you should attend to between, say, 9 a.m. and noon.

> *Politely ask the interviewer or someone at the target organization for a copy of the formal description of the job you'll be trying to win. This is easily the most important part of your morning. If you can, get the company to fax a copy of the job description to you. (You will be spending some time at the library today; do a little research and find out the fax number of a copy center located nearby. Ask the company to send the written job description there, and pick up the fax before you head to the library.)*

You shouldn't feel at all hesitant about asking for this. If you handle the call correctly, you won't come across as pushy, only as someone who is eager to prepare as thoroughly as possible. That's an attractive trait! In the unlikely event that there is no written description for the company to pass along, ask for a brief verbal summary of the duties of the position. Take this summary down verbatim.

While you're at it, you should ask for directions to the place where you'll be interviewing. If they are complex, or if you can't find anyone to pass them along to you, you should consult a third party and build in plenty of time to your schedule (at least one hour extra, perhaps an hour and a half extra) in which to get lost. *It is far preferable to have half an hour to kill before you enter the building than it is to show up even two or three minutes late for your interview.* Many prospective employers form indelible first impressions based on late arrivals.

Head to the library!

Settle in at the library. Take a half-hour to draw as many parallels as you can between your own experience and the specific requirements of the job. If you can, tie your success stories directly to aspects of the job for which you will be interviewing. If the job requires you to develop graphics on a computer system, for instance, and one of your success stories highlights your ability to deal with a number of different computer programs, including a word processing program with an extensive graphics function, you should make a note of this. In the available time, jot down the essentials in a notebook. (Writing these items down will help to reinforce them in your memory.)

Does your library feature an online reference service? If so, take a brief moment to punch in the name of your target company and see what comes up. If you are pointed toward an article or book, congratulations! You've hit the jackpot. Head to the stacks and take a look at the material.

Warning! It is extremely easy to get sidetracked when dealing with computer information systems! You have a limited amount of time, and you must use it wisely. If you see something *that isn't a direct reference to the company you're* looking for, but seems likely to be helpful later on in your research, *make a brief note of it and come back to it later. Your first aim is to take a few minutes to learn whether the library can* point you toward any *specific* information about *this* company.

After you've checked any online research aids that are available to you, you'll probably want to take a look at the *Reader's Guide to Periodical Literature* to check for any articles focusing on your target company. Find the articles (if there are any) first, then photocopy them for later review.

Is the company at which you'll be interviewing a publicly traded firm? If so, it issues an annual report to stockholders. Ask the librarian for help in tracking down this invaluable document, which includes specific information you need: mission statements, business segments, current business challenges and much more.

You're likely to find this report at the large libraries that serve major metropolitan areas—not the smaller branch facilities. If your target company issues an annual report, you owe it to yourself to track it down and read it carefully. (Call ahead to find out whether your library has the report.) If you find the annual report you're looking for, photocopy any relevant passages for later study.

The online research services and the *Reader's Guide to Periodical Literature* may point you toward articles about the target company; the listing of annual reports will let you know whether there are any reports on file for your firm.

Once you've gone through these two steps, and perhaps checked any available business-related reference guides likely to mention your target company (such as the *Million*

Dollar Directory), you will want to focus less on the specific company, and more on the particular industry.

Don't waste all morning in search of a citation that mentions your company by name; move on. You should briefly check the library's book catalog for any titles about your target company or its top leadership, but once you've taken a quick look, try to identify one or two relevant books that will reinforce or amplify your knowledge of the industry in general. Find the books you need, but don't settle in to your reading just yet. You have a limited amount of time, and you will need to focus on the most important information first.

Look for trade magazines relating to the industry within which you're interviewing. Yes, you will have stacked up quite a lot of material by now, but you will want to make one more appeal for information before you attack the mountain. Ask the librarian to point you toward the industry trade magazine of your target company. (If you are interviewing with a publisher, for example, you'll want to look at *Publishers Weekly*. If you are interviewing with an entertainment firm, you'll want to see *Variety*.)

If you can, secure the last seven to 10 of these magazines. *Scan* them for references to your target company. (Many of these magazines will incorporate quick-reference summaries and indexes that will make this task easier.) Remember that advertisements from your target company are just as worthy of study as editorial references to it.

In the time remaining to you, review and make notes on the materials you've set aside in the following rough order.

- Materials from or about your target company, including annual reports, articles that reference your target firm, interviews with top decision-makers and paid advertisements. *Review these materials closely, and take appropriate notes.* If you can, make photocopies, and highlight key points.

- Materials about the target company's industry, including trade magazines and books. Scan the table of contents or headlines for parts of the text you should review. Once again, photocopy any portions you can and highlight key elements.

- Other materials that have some bearing on your target company. You might, for instance, have come across an article that deals with a major supplier of your target company, or a book about the early history of the industry in question. These are optional resources only if you can't track down anything else, or if you've exhausted all your other materials and still have some time left.

Time's up! What's next?

Lunch. Don't skip it. For that matter, don't skip *anything* your body has gotten accustomed to over the years: sleep, for instance, or a shower, or the occasional break from your work. The fact that you're preparing for an interview doesn't mean the normal rules of sound health and hygiene have been suspended. In fact, they're more important than ever.

Take a break. Grab a sandwich. Relax for a half hour or, if you're feeling particularly drained, a full 60 minutes. Believe it or not, your interview preparation campaign will be better off as a result.

After your break, you must find someplace where you can speak freely, and where you won't be disturbed for at least three hours. By "not disturbed," I mean no ringing telephones, no kids asking questions about homework, no interruptions of any kind. If you have to camp out in a relative's spare guest room in order to win some solitary, talk-out-loud time, make the call and fold away the hide-a-bed. You're going to be practicing your responses to the most common interview questions, and you're going to be doing it out loud.

Why should you say your answers out loud? There are two reasons. First, you'll improve your delivery. As a direct result, you'll find yourself feeling more confident when it comes time to dealing with the questions in an actual interview setting. Second, saying the answers out loud ahead of time will help you in a way that mental repetition won't.

As you read the following advice on dealing with specific questions, develop your response as suggested, then repeat it out loud until you are satisfied with the result. (You may wish to use a tape recorder or video camera to monitor and review your delivery.)

As you rehearse your responses, please remember that the suggestions relating to particular questions, suggestions that appear throughout this book, are meant to be used to help you develop a unique, spontaneous response to the query posed. It is not in your interest to develop an answer that runs along at such a breakneck pace that it sounds as though it must have been memorized word-for-word. Nor should you deliver your response in an unvarying monotone. The aim is to project an image of preparedness, not a talent for simple repetition.

> *Prepare yourself for some variation on the question, "Tell me about yourself." Don't wing it. It's trickier than it looks, and it is definitely worth preparing for. This wide-open query may be an innocuous conversation-starter. More likely, it may be a shrewd attempt on the part of the interviewer to gather key facts about your self-image, your priorities and the way you are likely to respond to a request from a superior.*

Many people see this question listed in books and think, "Oh, that's no problem. I can handle a question like that without wasting a lot of time preparing for it." Don't make that mistake. It's easy to underestimate how intimidating this request can be. But if you don't prepare for it, this one can leave you babbling for several minutes about irrelevant school plays, "good people skills" or how little you like your present job or supervisor. (Any doubts as to whose side the interviewer is going to take in that little drama?)

Your best bet here is to use the question as an opportunity to send the message that you are excited about the work you do—and to drop a few tantalizing hints to the prospective employer about your ability to adapt well to *new systems,* take a *market-oriented approach* and keep an eye out for *the bottom line.* If those concepts don't sound familiar, go back to Chapter 1! These are the three ideas behind the personal anecdotes you developed earlier in the book.

Stay away from full-scale success stories right now. You and the interviewer are just getting the ball rolling. If you are asked for proof of your aptitudes or accomplishments in the areas you outline, you'll earn points for answering specifically. Emphasize your passionate interest in the industry and offer some corroborating evidence for this interest (perhaps by referring to some of the research you recently conducted). Then move along to the three points mentioned previously. What you say could sound something like this:

"Well, Ms. Jones, I've been following the rare book business very closely for some time, and I'm extremely excited about the prospect of working in it. I've been reading about a new auction in Boston at which one of Shakespeare's Second Folios will go on sale, and I thought that was certainly an event I'd want to attend—not that I can afford to buy the book, of course! I'd just like to take a look at something that historic in person.

*"Beyond that, I'd say I deal well with changes,
whether they're in technology or organizations, or in
the rare book market. I deal well with customers and
can spot new opportunities for sales, and I know how
important personal and organizational efficiency is to
the organization's bottom line."*

A response like this—when delivered in a casual, upbeat style that doesn't sound canned—will go a long way toward establishing a positive first impression, one that the interviewer is likely to remember. (Don't forget, you are competing with others for this job. Let them be the ones to ramble on at length about their favorite pets.) If you handle this common first question correctly, you will have a shot at determining the entire later structure of the interview!

Many (but not all) hiring managers start out with this question simply because they can't think of anything else to ask. If you offer an answer along the lines of the one I've just outlined, you'll offer this uncertain questioner a natural follow-up: "Really? Can you give me an example of a time when you adapted well to a new situation?" Fortunately, that's a question you're well-prepared to answer!

This situation arises more often than you think! Once you consider that at least half of the people who conduct job interviews have no particular aptitude for the task, you'll realize how important preparing your success stories is. Having a sense of what you want to get accomplished at the interview—which is not the same thing as *taking over* the interview—may be enough in and of itself to help you win the notice of a bored or incompetent questioner.

"Why are you thinking of leaving your current job?"

Prepare yourself for this question or some variation of it. You are likely to encounter it during any serious job interview. Its a pretty simple underlying message: *No real problems to speak of in the past, but now it's time to move on and try to achieve bigger and better things.*

> *You* must not *criticize your current or previous employer, even if you are specifically invited to do so by the interviewer. (That's a common interview trap, by the way.) Keep the tone positive and focus on the future. Keep your answer brief.*

If you are currently employed, your answer could sound something like this:

"I've done some wonderful things at McCall Associates over the past two years, and I've certainly learned a lot there. It will be difficult to say good-bye to Walt Powers, my supervisor—he and I have always gotten along very well—but I've come to the conclusion that the opportunities for growth there just aren't in line with my current skills. I'm eager to move into a position where I can make a more meaningful contribution in the design area on a day-to-day basis, not just once or twice a month."

If you were laid off, say so openly and don't apologize for your current employment status. Your experience is one that is, as of this writing, shared by thousands of American workers *every week*. There is no blame or failure to explain or acknowledge on your part. Explain what happened and adapt the basic message to fit your own situation.

"You may have heard about the layoff that took place at Fritz-Fallon earlier this year. I was one of the managers they let go, despite the fact that I had

*received an 'excellent' rating on my performance
evaluation just three months before. It's been an
interesting stretch of time, but in a way I think I've
been able to focus more clearly than I could have on
some new product ideas that I think are going to
make someone a lot of money. I've been kicking
around a couple of very exciting concepts in the
months since I left my old employer."*

By the way, this answer can also be adapted without
too much difficulty to a situation in which you are return-
ing to the job market after a long personal period off.

If you were fired, don't duck the issue. Say what happened
when you are asked about your previous position, and explain
what you learned from the event. *Don't* insist that you were
right and that the employer was wrong. Make it clear that
you understand that life is a process of growth and change,
and that this change, like any other, had lessons for you.
Your attitude toward the event may play just as large a
role as the specifics of the incident.

Be honest, but place the experience in the proper perspective. Emphasize individual *events* rather than ongoing
patterns that led to your dismissal. Your interviewer will be
trying to determine whether you are likely to be a problem
employee.

Take the time you need to make it clear that you have
a solid grasp of what happened and what you gained from
the experience, but don't spend an inordinate amount of
time justifying yourself. If you were able to secure a written recommendation from your employer, you should offer
to supply this to the interviewer at the end of your answer.

If you *don't* have a written letter of recommendation
from your previous employer, you should consider asking
for one. If it's impossible to offer to pass along a solid written recommendation to your interviewer, simply address

the issue of your firing in a straightforward way and then focus on the future in an optimistic way.

"I was discharged from my previous position because I had a dispute with my boss about a sales territory I thought I was entitled to, a dispute I mishandled badly. It was a difficult experience for me, but I learned a lot from it, and I've done a lot of thinking in the time since about the best ways to approach these kinds of questions.

"Looking back on it now, I have to say that I let my desire to achieve at a high level keep me from paying attention to some signals I should have been picking up on during that discussion, and I think I'm a better salesperson today for having learned that lesson.

"Right now, I'm looking for an opportunity to make a powerful contribution to a sales staff, and I know that when I find that opportunity I'll bring a good deal of valuable experience to the table that will keep things running smoothly for everyone."

"Would you have difficulty adapting to this environment?"

This question is most likely to arise when you are trying to make the transition from a small organization to a large one, or vice versa. And in settings where the interviewer is interested in your ability to deal with differing viewpoints and opinions.

The trap you must avoid is obvious enough: simply answering no, without offering any supporting details. Nothing will confirm the interviewer's suspicion that you're on your own private wavelength than a one-syllable response to a question that is clearly intended to get you to open up on the subject of your communication style.

Last Minute Interview Tips

This is the perfect opportunity for you to display your flexibility when it comes to dealing with other people. Share one of the success stories you have developed that deals with this trait.

"No, I really don't think so. You know, I've found over the years that I have a very good aptitude for dealing with new situations and new ideas. That's one of the points that's come up on several occasions in my performance reviews. I actually was able to use a quote from my supervisor along these lines on my resume. She said something to the effect that if she had a department full of people like me, implementing new procedures and training people in new systems would be a lot easier.

"Let me give you an example of the kind of flexibility I'm talking about. My supervisor was behind schedule on a couple of her own projects, and she desperately needed some rewrites and corrections on a training manual that had to go to the printer the next day. I was quite comfortable with the notion of taking a stab at clarifying things, but there was a problem—the manual had been entered into a complicated graphics program, not into our standard word processor, and I had no experience dealing with the new program.

"My superior gave me a copy of the manual, asked me to look it over and told me to get back in touch with her if I wasn't finished with the job within eight hours. I completed it in six, and learned the program as I went along. My boss had two extra hours to review my work, and the manual went off to the printer on schedule. My supervisor thought it looked great, and I have to admit that I did, too."

"What makes you so great?"

Prepare yourself for this type of question. An experienced interviewer will ask this question to gauge your self-confidence and poise, and may even phrase it in an overtly challenging way in an effort test your mettle. Such "stress questions" may be phrased in the following ways:

- "I've heard nothing but bad things about the people who graduated from your college. Why should you be any different from any of the others who've been through here?"
- "I have to be honest. This resume really doesn't do much for me. Why should I hire you?"
- "What makes you any better than the 30 other people I've talked to about this job?"

A less-seasoned interviewer may resort to "What makes you so great?" questions in a desperate attempt to get you to assume control of the interview process. These queries may sound a good less intimidating than stress questions:

- "What do you think is the greatest strength you'd bring to a job like this?"
- "Why should I consider you to be the strongest applicant for this opening?"
- "What would you consider to be your strong suit in performing a job like this?"

In both cases, your objective will be to maintain your poise, ignore the challenge (if any) implicit in the question, and fire off one or more of your success stories. And send silent signals to the interviewer who is lobbing you softballs that you are more than happy to supply intelligent, purposeful answers even to vague or incomprehensible questions.

Here's one way you might go about addressing a "show-me-you're-the-best-candidate-for-the-job" query, one that incorporates a not-so-subtle slur on your *alma mater.*

The success story adapted is one highlighting flexibility when dealing with new systems and procedures.

"Well, I'm not sure I know enough about the experiences you may have had with other Collins graduates to shed any light there, but for my own part I think I bring exactly the kinds of qualities to this job that your organization seems to be looking for.

"From what I understand, a major part of success in this job is in helping to develop presentations for potential clients for your agency. I've mastered a good many computer software programs in the past in order to set up some proposals that won major contracts, including work with Highlight Publishers and MacMaster Books.

"My last supervisor made a point of praising my ability to deal with a number of graphics programs in putting this work together. I'm confident I'd be able to develop visually striking materials that could win business for this firm, too."

"What's your greatest weakness?"

This question may make you wonder how on earth *you* can get a job interviewing people for open positions. How much wit is required to pose a question like this? What can the interviewer possibly gain by asking you to detail your flaws? Does he or she really expect you to roll over and play dead by listing them in detail?

This simplistic query may be used by an experienced interviewer to probe your inventiveness when dealing with a peculiarly phrased direct question, one that basically puts you in an impossible position: "Make your case for winning this job by telling me why you aren't qualified for it." In such cases, your ability to react to conflict situations without losing your cool is being probed as much as (or more than) the facts that underlie your answer.

Poor interviewers may ask this question because they really do expect you to outline any potential mismatches, or because they're in a foul mood. Respond to any queries with an answer that emphasizes your fixation on quality or performance issues and places any problems firmly in the past tense, such as:

"I suppose my greatest weakness would probably have some connection with an old habit of mine—of expecting everyone to spot mistakes the same way I do, or to put in the same effort, time, or energy I think necessary to complete a project on time and to everyone's satisfaction.

"A few years back, I realized that I often expected my colleagues to pay attention to these issues on the same terms that I did, but I've realized that everyone has a different approach to dealing with quality-control and deadline issues, and that mine is just a little more intense than that of many of my co-workers.

"I've had no problems interacting with others on day-to-day issues since I made this adjustment to my own style, but I make a note of reminding myself about it every once in a while all the same."

"What do you see yourself doing five years from now?"

Knowing what you want is a very attractive quality. Without going overboard and saying something along the lines of, "I'd like to have your job," you should find a way to demonstrate your certainty and confidence in the direction you've established for yourself and your personal level of comfort with the industry you've selected. *Do not* say that have no idea where you will be five years from now. *Do not* say that you may or may not be working in the industry your target company occupies five years from now.

Your answer should probably sound similar to this one. Note that it incorporates a bottom-line oriented success-story at the conclusion!

> *"I definitely see myself working within the advertising industry five years from now, and I'd like to think there's a good chance I'd be making a contribution here at Gerhard and Wilder. My main aim is to help develop campaigns that result in significant market advances for the clients involved, and that's certainly an aim I can see working toward in this position, and perhaps later in a more senior role within the agency.*

> *"The main thing I want to do over the next five years, no matter what title I hold, is to help develop arresting, creative ways of reaching potential consumers, and to deliver significant revenue to my company in the process.*

> *"I think Gerhard and Wilder is the perfect place to develop my existing skills in that regard, although I think I've made a pretty good start in my current position. As I mentioned to you over the phone, I was able to develop a campaign that helped to move Radial Tire of Worcester from third place in its market to first."*

"Do you have any questions before we conclude?"

This "wrap-up" question, perhaps the most common query in the world of interviewing, is botched by a high percentage of the people to whom it is posed.

You should not say "No," and smile contentedly in the interviewer's direction. This may be the typical response to the inquiry that marks the end of the main phase of the interview. "No" is a mindless answer that serves only to demonstrate to the employer that you are eager to get out of the batter's box, even if that means passing up a fat pitch down the heart of the plate.

You should not ask about salary, benefits, perks, vacation time or what the interviewer thought of your performance during the interview. Any query along these lines will only serve to make the interviewer uncomfortable. Asking about compensation-related issues before an offer has been extended has the added disadvantage of undermining your negotiation position; the employer can simply respond with something like, "Well, that depends—what are you looking for?" Let the employer raise the issue of compensation.

So what should you say? There are two good options: First, you can raise an intelligent question based on your library research, one that shows that you have an interest in following the industry in which the target company operates. Your question could sound like this:

"Yes, I do have a question. I noticed in your annual report that your company is hoping to develop full-scale bank-by-modem access for your customers by the middle of next year. I thought that was very exciting. Do you know if that initiative is still on?"

It could also sound like this.

"I read in Business Week *that your company's revenues have grown by at least 40 percent in each of the past six years. That's a pretty remarkable record; what do you think is the main reason for your success?"*

Keep it simple; don't pepper the interviewer with technical questions to which he or she may not know the answer. Use your question as an expression of interest and appreciation, and as a signal of the research you've done on the target organization.

The other option—one to incorporate in your research-based questioning—sounds something like this:

"Yes. Ms. Smith, I have to tell you, I'm very excited about the prospect of working for your firm as an account executive. I've done a good deal of research on your organization and, to tell you the truth, I am now deeply committed to the goal of working here. I've got one question that's more important to me than any other: What do I have to do to win this job, so I can start making a contribution here as a full-time employee as soon as possible?"

This is, of course, what's known as taking the direct approach, and some job seekers are more likely to be comfortable asking a question like this than others. Before you dismiss this approach outright, however, let me assure you that by confidently asking a question like this at the conclusion of your interview, you will set yourself apart from *90 out of 100* of the people who are competing with you for the job. If your interview has not gone as well as you'd like, this question may revive your prospects. If your interview *did* go well, this question may close the deal for you.

Whatever approach you choose to take in responding to the "Do you have any questions" query, ask between one and three intelligent, nonthreatening, confident questions, then follow the interviewer's lead and let the interview come to a close.

Now what?

You've done your research, studied your success stories, and prepared answers to the seven interview questions explored in this chapter. Now what? Briefly *review* your research from the morning's library work. The idea is to have a general familiarity with the most important items, so that you can inject them *in a natural way* into the conversation when and if the occasion arises.

Once you've done that, you should call it a day. As a matter of fact, no matter *what* you've gotten accomplished so far today, you should call it a day if it's now close to dinnertime. Take the time you need to eat a square meal and stop working on your preparation for your interview. Unwind. Clear your head. Pick out that sharp outfit you're going to wear tomorrow. Remind yourself that the first and most important asset you will be bringing to the interview tomorrow is yourself.

Don't spend all night feverishly preparing for questions. If you're tossed a tough question during the interview, one that really throws you for a loop, you have two great options for dealing with it. Here they are:

- Find some way to tie in the question to one of your success stories.
- Admit you don't know the answer to the question posed. Explain that it's simply out of your experience base, and let your interviewer know that if you came across such an issue in a work setting, you'd appeal to a superior for guidance. This answer is perhaps not quite as attractive as the first option, and it is *not to be appealed to more than once* during the interview. But it is a valid and often effective response nonetheless.

If your interviewer is like most of the people who have to evaluate potential new hires, he or she spends a great deal of time listening to people explain that they can handle any crisis, respond to any challenge, and work any miracle, 24 hours a day. By acknowledging with disarming honesty that you *don't* know it all, and that you appreciate the necessity of appealing to experience now and then, you may be able to win points. You will be, after all, handling the question in exactly the way a good professional should when assessing an unfamiliar set of facts: admitting the limitations of one's knowledge without getting flustered about those limitations.

You've given the job of preparing for the interview your best shot. Your job now is to make sure you look and feel your best when the meeting itself rolls around. Eat well; get enough sleep. Tomorrow morning, be sure to groom yourself carefully before the interview. See Chapter 8 for a full listing of important pre-interview tasks.

Now, you're ready to dazzle!

Chapter 4

If you have an interview in 2 to 3 days

Things aren't exactly scheduled perfectly, but time isn't *quite* so tight in this situation. You don't have to call in sick at your current job, corral family members into baby-sitting for you with no advance notice or beg the reference librarian for research help during one feverish morning. You've got all of half a work week to prepare for this interview. You may even be able to squeeze in a weekend day or two as well. That means you can take things at a somewhat more leisurely pace when it comes to research—and prepare in depth for a few more of the most common interview questions.

What's my first stop?

The main branch of your local library, of course. You're going to be able to spend at least (gasp!) a whole day, and hopefully a day-and-a-half, at this fine institution, so commit to doing exactly that. If at all possible, you should commit to a full day, and to a full 9 a.m.-to-noon slot the following morning, doing *nothing else but conducting your research work at the library.*

Yes, you really should set aside an entire uninterrupted day or day-and-a-half for this work. It's worth noting that the vast majority of the people with whom you will be competing for the job will not expend even the most basic effort finding out about the prospective employer or the industry.

By making a firm pledge to devote time to the task of finding out about the world as it's perceived by your prospective employer, you will be putting yourself at an advantage.

Remember that a fair number of the people who walk in the door for a professional interview have little or no idea about the specifics of the job, or the prospective employer's products or services, or the competitive challenges faced by the organization. *Because of this sad fact, the interviewer will in all likelihood have come to the silent assumption that you are like these applicants, before having exchanged a word with you!*

You must, during the course of the interview, tactfully rectify this misimpression. The best way to do this is to spend *sustained, uninterrupted time beforehand* at the library focusing on the essential research questions outlined in this chapter.

Let's assume that you have already developed the success stories discussed in detail in Chapter 1. (If you haven't, make that the first item on your list as you walk into the library, and adjust the rest of your schedule accordingly.) Your priority list will look something like this:

Job one: Draw parallels between your background and the job. See Chapter 3 for suggestions on obtaining the job description if you have not already done so. The more parallels you can make between the specific requirements of the open position and your own past work or volunteer experience, the better. During the interview, you should be familiar enough with the requirements to cite the parallels directly. (You will not, of course, raise for discussion any area where your experience is less than that required for the position.)

Depending on the amount of time available to you, you will probably want to spend at least one hour, perhaps as much as two hours, developing these parallels *in writing* and associating key requirements of the job description with the success stories you've already developed. Writing the points down will help you reinforce them in your own memory and will make it easier for you to cite the appropriate connections when the opportunity arises during the interview.

Job two: Check for articles about the company. If your library is relatively large, it may have an online article search service that will make this an easy process. You simply enter the company name (or the name of a top officer) as a key word and wait to see what the computer brings up in the way of citations. The librarian will help point you in the right direction when it comes to tracking down any articles referenced.

Today's online reference databases and computerized article archives are amazingly powerful research tools. It's worth tracking down a large metropolitan library that offers these resources, even if it means traveling a little further than you otherwise might.

If you can't locate a library that offers these tools, or if you feel like augmenting your computerized research with an article or two from a time period that predates the library's database, you'll probably want to track down the appropriate volume of the *Reader's Guide to Periodical Literature* and check the appropriate index headings.

Job three: Look for annual reports. As noted earlier, all publicly held companies issue annual reports. If your target company is privately held or a nonprofit organization, you shouldn't waste time trying to track down a report to stockholders.

If your target organization *does* issue an annual report, try to get hold of one. It will feature a whole host of important facts, including the various divisions of the operation, details about the company's current financial status and competitive challenges, and mission statements or other important text that will point you toward the company's guiding philosophy.

Job four: Track down the trade magazines. An intelligent review of your target organization's trade magazine is a must if you wish to be perceived as someone who has an idea of what's going on in the industry. Given the amount of time at your disposal, I'd recommend perusing between 10 and 12 of the most recent issues. Simply browse your way through them, as you would any other magazine, making note of points likely to affect decision-makers in this industry.

Many people try to skip this step, and it's easy to understand why. A good many of the magazines in question are not particularly thrilling reading to outsiders. Some are not laid out well. Some are not written well. But let me answer these objections by posing a simple question: Would you rather be perceived as an outsider or as an insider?

The question is particularly important for you to ponder if you are searching for your first position in the industry. As I've mentioned before in this book, employers very quickly develop a sense of who possesses that elusive passion, especially when evaluating the potential of applicants who are hoping to break into a competitive field without the benefit of experience in the industry in question.

Enthusiasm is fine, but knowledge of current trends and events in your interviewer's industry is a necessary complement to that enthusiasm. In fact, these two aspects of your candidacy are really two sides of the same coin. If you're enthusiastic about the industry in general, but are so vague in your enthusiasm that you have no concrete facts about which to express your ardor, you shouldn't expect to get far during your interview. By the same token, if you possess a strong technical knowledge of a particular type of business operation, but can't seem to develop much passion about the larger issues the company faces, you may do your candidacy a disservice.

Pay attention to both sides of the equation. Take appropriate time to review the most recent issue of the trade publication directly targeted toward your organization's industry. If you can't find *anything* in that publication to hold your interest, there's a very good chance you're trying to win a job in the wrong industry!

Just a reminder: You have a significant amount of research time at your disposal (ideally, a day to a day-and-a-half). Make sure you touch all the bases, allotting appropriate amounts of time to each of the steps discussed in this chapter. Don't skip steps. Budget your precious library time intelligently. The more balanced your approach, the more likely you are to be able to cite a particular part of your research confidently during your discussions with the interviewer.

What now?

If you find that you've been able to make solid progress on all of the items listed previously, you should use whatever remaining time you have at the library to pursue one more objective: *researching one of the target company's own customers,* or, failing that, taking time to determine the average profile of that customer. With the hour or two still at your disposal after you've made all your notes and photocopied all your documents, you should ask yourself: What, specifically, would I be well-advised to know about this company's customers if I ended up working at the firm?

At some companies, the idea will be to identify the one or two entities that constitute the principal source of income for the target organization. If you're going to be interviewing at a software development firm, for instance, your objective would be to identify and learn more about the two or three main software retailers likely to do business with that firm.

At other companies, your objective will be to develop a profile of the typical consumer likely to order directly from the company. If you'll be interviewing for a job as the manager of a local bookstore, you'll want to gain a deeper understanding of the average income, likely level of education and purchasing patterns of the areas from which the store draws its customers.

This is often an easier task than it sounds. Ask the librarian to point you toward any demographic surveys or articles that will throw light on the organization's consumers.

You may also decide to try to track down an advertisement from your target employer. What publication or medium does the advertisement appear in? What types of people are likely to read it? What tone does the advertisement take in addressing its audience? The answers to these questions will tell you a lot about the people your target organization is trying to reach.

The idea is to take the extra hour or so that may be at your disposal and find a way to answer the question, "What kinds of customers does this company consider to be most important?" Whether the answer is one or two huge corporations or government entities, or teenagers who buy three or more pairs of athletic shoes every 12 months, you should note the answers and be prepared to work them into your responses at appropriate points during the interview.

Once you wrap up your uninterrupted library research, you should head home and give yourself a chance to unwind. Remember that eating well, resting when you need to, selecting professional-looking interview clothing and maintaining good personal hygiene is part of sound interview preparation.

Prepare for the interview questions

During your interview, it's a good bet you'll need to address one or more of the following interview questions:

- "Tell me about yourself."
- "Why are you considering leaving your current position?" Or "Why did you leave your previous position?"
- "Would you have difficulty adapting to the way we do things around here?"
- "What's your greatest strength?"
- "What's your greatest weakness?"
- "What do you see yourself doing five years from now?"
- "Do you have any questions before we wrap up?"

Strategies for dealing with these extremely common interview queries appear in Chapter 3. Be sure you develop customized, spontaneous-sounding responses to each, and practice all of them *out loud*. Then do the same for the following questions:

"How has your job search been going?"

Is it really relevant to the interviewer's purposes whether you've been in job search mode for one week or six months? Well, yes and no.

Yes, because how long you've been looking may be perceived, erroneously, as a sign of your employability (or, perhaps, your level of desperation).

No, because any attempt you make to secure employment will be affected by any number of factors that the interviewer probably has neither the time nor the inclination to discuss: your other time commitments, any changes in strategy that you may have implemented, offers that fell through at the last minute, and so on.

Last Minute Interview Tips

I'm the last person on earth to encourage you to lie to an interviewer, but this is one situation where you are best advised to leave at least the implication that your job search is a relatively young one. Once you've done so, you should probably change the subject and focus on one of your strong suits.

Leaving the prospective employer with the impression that you've been pounding the pavement for months may encourage him or her to think that other companies know something about you that isn't obvious on the surface.

Your best strategy here is to briefly, but confidently, appeal to other job offers you've received, even modest ones, if you can possibly do so. You should then cite the *direct parallels between your own job experience and the formal or informal job description you worked up in the library.* As a general rule, you will probably be perfectly within your rights saying something like this:

"It's been going quite well. I've gotten an offer from one company, but I didn't think the match was quite right, so I took a pass on it. Actually, I'm glad I did, because now I'm in a position to end up here, which is where I want to be. I think there's the potential for an excellent match here.

"From what I understand about the job description, you're looking for someone with two years of customer experience, and I've got two-and-a-half. You're looking for someone who can prioritize many tasks, which is exactly what I'm doing in my current position. And you're looking for someone who can train others to make sense of new systems, and I've conducted plenty of training in my work with volunteers during my present employer's fundraising broadcasts."

Don't lie about job offers you've received; your interviewer may well be able to determine a bluff easily with just a few deft questions. (More important, of course, is the core principle of making truthful statements, which is the best roadmap to follow on the job search.) If you haven't received an offer, you may want to respond with something like this before outlining the parallels between your own experience and the job description:

> *"It's been going very well indeed. I feel very lucky to have been able to set up a meeting with you! I thought it would take me a lot longer to get to this point."*

"Why should we assume you'll stick around for a while if we hire you?"

Many people have made the mistake of reading the "conditional hire" assumption embedded in this question as a signal that the hiring process has already concluded—and in their favor. Actually, this is a fairly common question that a good many employers tend to ask very early in the process. The guiding idea behind it is not, "You look great—promise us you'll stick around," but rather, "Why should I bother even talking to you if your resume leads me to believe you'll head out the door in a year?"

Your interviewer may ask you directly to explain why you've moved from one employer to another so often, or he or she may ask pointedly which of your jobs lasted the longest and why.

However the query is phrased, it is a reflection of the understandable concern on the part of the employer. Hiring and training an employee is an expensive, time-consuming proposition, one that the organization is unlikely to take on any more than it has to. Your job is to convince the prospective employer that you've put a good deal of thought into

the matter, and that you are eager to find a situation—
namely, this one—where you can grow over a period of time.
The more independent research you can cite to support this
claim, the better. You must show the interviewer that you
have a strong sense of why you have decided that *this* industry and *this* business make sense for you now.

If your resume features a good deal of company- or career-
hopping, your response could use a focus, such as:

> *"Although I've had to spend a few years in the*
> *software industry to find this out, I've come to the*
> *conclusion that publishing is the area that makes the*
> *most sense for me for at least the next three to five*
> *years or so. I say this because I think the opportunities*
> *for growth in your company are stronger than those of*
> *the company I'm at now, and also because I've had the*
> *opportunity to follow your industry over a period of*
> *time, and I like what I see your house doing.*

> *"I think that as a software manager I've gotten a very*
> *good sense of how and why people buy software books.*
> *Your line of books appeals to people who find the*
> *manuals that engineers develop to be a little*
> *intimidating. You've been able to emphasize a truly*
> *user-friendly approach to making sense of a new*
> *system, and you've been able to highlight that in your*
> *titles, in your graphic layout and in your advertising.*

> *"By the way, I should admit that it's no accident that*
> *bookstore consumers feel the way they do. The*
> *manuals that engineers develop* are *intimidating, and*
> *I've been agitating for some time to try to make them*
> *less so. I think I'd be in a better position to develop*
> *instruction products people can really sink their teeth*
> *into if I were working at a company like yours."*

"What strengths and weaknesses did your supervisor identify on your most recent performance review?"

Job seekers are well-advised to minimize past problems and maximize past successes when addressing a question such as this one. No matter how charming, endearing or charismatic your interviewer may be, you must remember that you are talking to someone who is evaluating your qualifications in a professional setting, not to a family member or a kindly representative of the clergy. You may want to answer a question in this category along the following lines:

"My last evaluation mentioned the fact that I have a tendency to take on too much, and I certainly realize that time management is an important part of performing well on a professional level.

"Actually, since that review, I've gotten quite a lot out of a book on time management that my supervisor passed along to everyone in the department, and I really don't think this area represents much of a problem for me now.

"As for the other side of the ledger, my boss mentioned my ability to handle many tasks simultaneously, my strong writing and design skills and my ability to adapt well to new situations and systems. One example of that would be my performance on the Fisk Industries project, where I had to develop an entirely new method of evaluating a client's projected inventory demands by using a new piece of software for which no owner's manual existed yet! The president of the client firm said it was the sharpest piece of forecasting she'd ever seen. That made my supervisor pretty happy, and I guess I'd be less than honest if I said it didn't make me pretty happy, too."

"What don't you like about your current boss?" or *"What did you like least about your old boss?"*

It is *never* in your best interest to criticize a former (or present) employer during an employment interview. Even if there really were personality problems on the part of management, even if you really were subjected to questionable treatment, even if everyone else in the department thought of your supervisor as a tyrant *and had good reason to do so,* your conversational partner in an interview setting will virtually always take the employer's side of the situation.

Save the acrimony and accusations for private discussions with your close friends. For now, find a way to turn this potentially devastating question into another opportunity to accentuate the positive. In the following example, note how you send the interviewer the attractive message that the only thing you had against your previous supervisor was his occasional failure to take advantage of your desire to learn.

> *"Well, to tell you the truth, I genuinely liked working with Charlie. I didn't really have anything major in the way of complaints about our relationship. If I had to identify one habit of his that I thought could have been pointed in another direction, though, it would probably be the fact that he could sometimes take a while to share his knowledge with us when we were trying to make sense of some perplexing situations.*
>
> *"There were a few occasions I can think of where I'd ask for help in a certain area, and he'd promise to get right back to me on it and then his schedule would sort of overwhelm him. But that only happened a few times. For the most part, I'd say we had a great working relationship."*

"Why should we hire you?"

It's the simple questions that often throw you. Many an applicant has stammered and stuttered his or her way through an unconvincing response to this wide-open invitation to sell strong points.

Fortunately, if you've followed the advice in Chapter 1 and developed success stories that illustrate your flexibility, your market orientation and your bottom-line awareness, you've got this question licked.

"You should hire me for three reasons: For one thing, I adapt well to new systems and procedures. One example of that would be my performance during the hurricane two years ago, when we were short on staff and I had to take over the company's main switchboard without the benefit of any training so I could route emergency calls that were coming into our facility. I did so on my own and without any problem after about only 10 minutes of trial and error.

"The second reason you should hire me is that I have a solid sense of your company's customer base, and I know what kinds of services that customer base is looking for. The truth is, I represent a kind of walking focus group for your company; I've been a loyal subscriber to your network for the past three years, and I think I can help you develop new approaches from a customer-first standpoint.

"The third reason you ought to give me this job is that I understand that the reason the company opens its doors in the morning is so that it can turn a profit. My last three performance reviews at my current position made a point of mentioning my high personal efficiency, and I'd like to put that efficiency to work for your organization.

"Those are the three main reasons you ought to hire me, Ms. Hamilton, and I can guarantee you that if you do, you won't regret it."

"What's your management philosophy?"

If you're applying for a management position, you will need to develop an answer to this question that makes it clear that you know how to delegate, how to motivate and when to give credit where credit is due. You should, at all costs, stay away from answers that make vague appeals to your "ability to get along well with people."

By the same token, you must avoid leaving the interviewer with the impression that you believe the first and most important step to becoming a good manager is to get others to be your friends so they'll work harder on the projects you assign.

Your answer may sound like the one following. Note the incorporation of a success story that highlights your bottom-line orientation at the end.

"Well, when it comes right down to it, I believe that being a good manager means getting things done through others, and I try to provide the tools and the surroundings that make that process easy for everyone involved. Part of the manager's job is assembling teams and handing out assignments with a steadily more accurate sense of what combinations are likeliest to yield positive outcomes for the organization. Part of that task is trial and error, but part of it is making clear to team members that they're working in an environment where people are going to be judged on the basis of the results they deliver, and where they usually have some input into decisions that affect them.

"My experience is that if you make it clear that this is the kind of workplace you're trying to develop, people work hard and develop a strong sense of loyalty toward the organization.

"Let me give you an example of what I mean. At my current position, I had to get my team members to commit to an extremely aggressive deadline for a proposal. Instead of lecturing them about the importance of putting in extra hours, I outlined the goal we were looking at and told them about the time constraints we were working under. Then I broke them up into two teams and asked them to take 20 minutes to develop some ideas for how to approach the proposal. As it turned out, both teams came up with elements that were strong enough to incorporate into the final approach.

"Because all the individuals had a certain investment in the process at this point, they volunteered to stay late a few nights that week, and the proposal came out looking very sharp indeed. And it won us a $250,000 contract, a fact I made sure my superiors knew about when it came time to give salary reviews to the team members who'd put the proposal together. That story says as much about my management philosophy as anything, I think."

"What salary level are you looking for?"

The best way to approach this common question? Dodge it. It is not in your interests to discuss specific salary figures until the employer makes an offer. If you are pushed to the wall on the issue (probably a pretty good sign in and of itself), you should respond with a *vague* figure that eliminates as few options as possible. You might consider saying something like this:

"Well, my research leads me to believe that the average pay for this position in this industry can vary widely—from $20,000 per year up to $50,000 or more. But it all depends on the company and the individual, of course."

But you're better off sticking with something like this if you possibly can:

"I'm looking for a competitive compensation package that will take into account the many contributions I can make to a company like yours. From what I've heard about your organization, I don't have any doubt that we could work out a fair arrangement once an offer is on the table."

Go get 'em!

If you've followed all the advice in this chapter, you're now ready to put all your hard work to the test. The only thing left on your list is to *take good care of yourself,* and make sure you come across as sharp as possible when it's time to show up for the interview itself. See Chapter 8 for an important checklist that will keep you from skipping some vitally important preinterview steps.

Chapter 5

If you have an interview in 4 to 7 days

How lucky can you get? You've got days and *days* to work with! Plenty of time to develop a top-drawer interview strategy for your target company.

We live in an era in which a week is a world of time. Whole new markets have been known to materialize in a week—and companies to serve them can come into existence (or vanish) just as quickly. With four to seven days at your disposal, you're in a perfect position to take dramatic action to boost the chances that your job interview will culminate in the offer you deserve.

First stop: the library!

In this chapter, the working assumption will be that it's within your power to set aside at least two, and preferably two-and-a-half, uninterrupted days at the library. Yes, it is vitally important that this time be laid out in your schedule as inviolable research time. Checking out an interesting book and bringing it home to review after dinner is nice, but it's no substitute for cloistering yourself away for the sole purpose of *learning what you have to learn in order to ace the interview*.

Block off the weekend. Get someone to help you by pitching in to watch the kids. Or head to the library right after your current job lets out, grab a sandwich and put in four solid hours (that's half a day, if you're counting). Do whatever it takes to win 16 to 20 uninterrupted hours of library time, and devote that time exclusively to the task of interview preparation.

Match your strengths to the job's requirements. What should you *do* during those hours? Glad you asked. Assuming you've already developed the personal success stories we discussed in Chapter 1, you should head to the biggest library you can and start out by setting up a list of parallels between your strengths and the formal (or informal) requirements of the position.

Learning exactly how the prospective employer defines this job and finding as many possible matches between your background and the requirements the prospective employer will be trying to fill are two essential prerequisites to a winning performance during a job interview. If you can't be bothered to find out what the employer expects you to do after you've been hired, you shouldn't expect to be asked to join the target organization.

See Chapter 3 for some ideas on how best to secure a copy of the written job description—or, failing that, how to get someone within the organization to help you sketch out some informal guidelines related to the job duties. Then sit down with a pad and pen at the library and develop as many parallels and connections as you can between your skill set and the tasks you would have to perform on the job.

Look for specific articles about the company. This is easiest, of course, if you have parked yourself at a major, centrally located metropolitan library, one with a significant number of periodicals on reserve and/or an online text-retrieval or referencing system.

Even if the library does not feature an extensive collection of newspapers and magazines, and does not boast an-up-to-date computerized article search tool, it will almost certainly have that old standby, the *Reader's Guide to Periodical Literature.*

While this resource may identify articles about the company, beware: If you're pointed toward a single article in an obscure journal that you must drive two hours to review at another library, you're probably better off proceeding to the next research step than hitting the road. Even though you've got the better part of a week to work with, one of the chief advantages of working at the library is that doing so *forces you to focus on the research tasks* you must undertake to prepare for your interview.

Are you interviewing with a publicly traded company? If so, you should try to track down a copy of the target organization's annual report. This invaluable document will outline all kinds of indispensable facts: business segments, mission statements, even the financial position of the company.

The annual report can provide you with a wealth of "insider" information, and represents yet another reason you should point yourself toward the biggest, most comprehensive library in your area. (Most smaller branch libraries won't be able to provide you with annual reports. Your best bet is probably to call ahead to determine the availability of any annual report you're looking for.)

Once your search for an annual report has either turned up what you're looking for or resulted in a dead end, you should probably check the library's main catalog. Look for any books that deal *directly* with either your target organization or the industry.

Review trade magazines. Reviewing 12 to 14 of the most recent back issues for key points is a good strategy, given the time available to you. Don't attempt to read the magazines word for word, but *do* keep an eye out for articles your prospective supervisor would be likely to stop and review.

If you are trying to overcome a skill or experience gap, careful review of the trade magazines relevant to your industry is the single best way to do so. By becoming conversant with the issues and trends facing top decision-makers, you will go a long way toward developing the "insider" persona that will help your interviewer look past questions relating to your work history or to formal job requirements.

Research the customers. You should also take time during the "library phase" of your research to identify the organization's likely customers. Does this company do most of its business with two or three companies? Does it target individual consumers? How does it canvass for new business? What can you learn from advertisements the target organization has placed in newspapers or magazines?

The answers to these questions may take a little while to track down. In fact, odds are that with most companies, you'll never be able to get a fix on *all* the potential purchasers of the products or services offered. But you will be able to use the library's resources to develop a solid profile of the most important people and institutions your potential employer depends on for business. Budget a chunk of your library time to develop this critical element of your information file.

Still have some time on your hands?

If you've made good progress toward all of the research goals outlined and still have time, you should spend an hour doing a little brainstorming on the following question: "What new products or services or new ways of doing things could this company benefit from?"

What you're hoping to do is spend *a little* time here developing some initial ideas on a potentially profitable new approach for the company to consider. The work you do now may serve to demonstrate that you've got more on the ball than the average applicant.

During the interview, you will follow the interviewer's lead and wait for the proper moment to incorporate your idea. It may come at the end of the session, when the interviewer asks you whether you have any questions. You could use this question as the launching pad for your new idea or procedure:

> *"Yes, Ms. Smith; I was wondering if your organization had ever considered developing a World Wide Web site that would allow users to search for e-mail addresses of friends and relatives. I was thinking about this the other day—many of the search engines out there have some really amazing traffic levels, but all they do is point people toward other web sites.*
>
> *"It occurred to me that your company might be able to develop just as much interest in a site devoted exclusively to helping people track down e-mail addresses and generating revenue by selling ad space on the site. What would you think the potential of a project like that would be?"*

Is there a possibility the organization will appropriate your idea without credit? Sure. But that's a possibility in any interview setting, and if you let the potential downside keep you from demonstrating your own creativity, you'll probably be doing your job search a disservice. Most interviewers will recognize your question for what it is—evidence that you know how to think, and that you're not afraid to speak up about a potential area of profitability or increased efficiency.

Review your strategies for interview questions

Because you've got the better part of a week to focus on interview preparation, you'll be able to cover a good many of the most common interview questions. In addition to the questions covered in this chapter, you should also prepare for these:

- "Tell me about yourself."
- "Why are you considering leaving your current position?"
- "Why did you leave your previous position?"
- "Would you have difficulty adapting to the way we do things around here?"
- "What's your greatest strength?"
- "What's your greatest weakness?"
- "What do you see yourself doing five years from now?"
- "Do you have any questions before we conclude?"
- "How has your job search been going?"
- "What don't you like about your current boss?"
- "Why should we hire you?"
- "What strengths and weaknesses did your supervisor identify for you on your most recent performance review?"
- "Why should we assume you'll stick around for a while if we hire you?"
- "What's your management philosophy?"
- "What kind of salary are you seeking?"

You will find strategies for dealing with all of these questions in Chapters 3 and 4. Take the time to develop customized responses to each, responses that don't sound "canned." Then practice all your answers *out loud.* You should do the same for these interview questions:

"How do you approach the job of making key decisions?"

This is trickier than it sounds. You must use all that library research on the target organization, any general knowledge about the industry and your own sense of this particular interviewer's priorities to make an intelligent assessment of the decision-making traits *that are likely to be valued most.*

Why can't you simply outline the decision-making process you adopted the last time you had to make a judgment call? Because the corporate culture, the requirements of the position you want to win and the interviewer's mindset may all be pointing in the other direction! Let's say your last big decision was one where you had to make a quick-and-dirty assessment of a time-sensitive dilemma, and let's say you acted as an autonomous team member in a rough-and-ready, risk-taking startup firm. Even if the decision you made turned out to be the correct one, this is probably *not* the story you want to pass along to a punctilious interviewer who is a senior official at a staid, conservative financial company—one that emphasizes extensive, multi-layered, multi-party review of statistical information before committing to any decision. At such an organization, boasting about your ability to "follow your instincts," "think on your feet" and "make the tough calls independently when circumstances demand" is probably a very bad idea.

Deciding which of your problem-solving abilities to highlight during a job interview can be a very difficult task. If you feel at all uncertain about the way you should proceed in dealing with this question, your best bet is probably to ask *confidently and briefly* for a little more information about the types of problems under discussion. But bear in mind that *how* you ask is vitally important.

Your delivery should make it clear that you're quite comfortable dealing with any and every problem that may come your way, and that you don't shirk from the responsibility of assessing a sudden setback and acting intelligently.

At the same time, you must send the message that you're eager to quantify the particulars of the situation when you're faced with unfamiliar challenges. Fortunately, the very act of asking this "what-kind-of-decision-are-we-talking-about" question will help you send that second message!

Here's one example of what your clarifying question might sound like:

> *"Well, that depends. If there's one thing I've learned over the years, it's that even a comfortable decision-making approach can backfire if it's applied to any and every situation. What kind of problem are we talking about?"*

The take-charge tone will let the entrepreneurs and front-line commanders know that you are quite capable of handling yourself just as assertively and confidently as they would in a tough spot. Your attempt to gather more information before proceeding will impress the accountants and engineers you may run into.

Pay close attention to the answer you receive to this question and base your decision on which aspect of your decision-making style to emphasize. You will probably do best at the interview by emphasizing either the creative, independent approach or the evidence-tracking, get-everyone-in-on-this method of handling key decisions. When in doubt, let the organization's corporate culture, as you perceive it, be your guide!

"What do you want from your next job?"

"Oh, just the usual—a fat expense account, the chance to travel to any overseas destination I feel is worth inspecting, a company car, and a salary that's only a dollar or two below that of my immediate superior."

You'd be surprised how many people tackle this simple question by reciting, in detail, all the perks they expect. It's nice to have a sense of the rewards you have in mind, but your candidacy will probably be better served by an answer that shows that you see your next job as a personal and professional challenge, not simply as an excuse to head out the door with a fat paycheck every week.

If you focus on monetary rewards to the exclusion of all other factors, your interviewer will be understandably concerned about your dedication to the job in the event that another opportunity with a slightly higher dollar figure arises. And raising the issue of perks, benefits and specific salary levels should be considered taboo until the employer makes you a specific offer or raises such topics him- or herself.

The big message to send to the prospective employer is a simple one: You want, first and foremost, to work at this company. Frame your answer accordingly, and make it clear how important it is for you to be challenged, to excel and to make a meaningful contribution.

"In my next job, I hope to be able to continue to grow as a trainer, and to be able to implement training systems that help my company's customers increase their revenues and their sales effectiveness. I feel it's important to work with the best, which is why I'm interviewing here, and I also feel that once you've hooked up with a company of the caliber of this one, it's essential that you make a commitment to personal excellence.

"That means making a long-term promise to develop and present effective sales training programs, spotting and taking advantage of any opportunities to improve, and accepting that, in the long run, the most enjoyable kind of work is the kind that has some challenge associated with it.

For me, that challenge is to be the best trainer I'm capable of being, and that translates into delivering tangible results for customers, results that leave them feeling that their time and money has been very well spent indeed."

"How do you approach personal time management?"

The prospective employees interviewers like to hire tend to demonstrate the following business traits:

- Ability to generate own motivating sense of purpose (independent, "low-maintenance" self-starter type).

- Capacity to prioritize intelligently, even when things are hectic.

- Willingness to get down to business (not a procrastinator).

Your answer (which may appeal to a bottom-line success story as it concludes) should draw as many connections as possible between your own work habits and the traits just outlined. It could sound something like this:

"Well, I can honestly say that I generally find a way to bring projects in on time and looking sharp. When unexpected circumstances interfere with progress on a project, I think I do a pretty good job of finding places where I can quickly make up the time that's been lost.

"One good way to keep schedules under control, I've found, is to develop a personal to-do list at the beginning of each day. During the course of the day, I add to the list or change my priorities as situations demand. I also make a point of finding time to devote my attention completely to an important task— without short-changing the needs of the people I work with, of course.

"On a recent project for my current supervisor, I showed up at 7:30 in the morning on two particular days so I could deliver the financial statements she needed to close out our annual reports, and still not miss any of the staff meetings. She told me that we avoided having to pay something like $4,000 in late fees to the printer because she got the material she needed, when she needed it."

"What's the most challenging situation you've ever faced?"

A variation might be, "Can you think of a time when it was more difficult to make things come out positively for everyone involved?" These sly questions, often phrased with a "we're-all-in-this-together" tone more reminiscent of a conversation between two colleagues than a professional interview, are designed to get you to open up about potential problem areas of your candidacy. Your response may reveal a weakness or conflict in your work style, and you may be eliminated from consideration.

Although such a response may make the interviewer's job a lot easier (by torpedoing your candidacy), it should go without saying that your response to this subtle twist on the "tell-me-your-greatest-weakness" question must feature some sensitivity to this ploy.

Last Minute Interview Tips

When outlining an instance that represents your greatest past challenge to a prospective employer, you should, if your background allows, incorporate an element from the following list:

- A time you had to fire someone, lay someone off or announce a downsizing. If you can truthfully point to such a situation, this should be the winner by a country mile. Nobody likes telling another person bad employment news like this. The interviewer will identify with your plight and respect the fact that you've made it through this management rite of passage. *Do not* imply that you enjoyed the act of letting the person in question go.

- A time you had to master a new system or procedure from scratch, with little or no help from management—but did.
- This is essentially an adaptation of one of your flexibility-related success stories. Emphasize the obstacles you faced and point out how you overcame them. Because the questioner is expecting a negative outcome of some kind, you may want to conclude by pointing out how you had to take time away from other pressing obligations, and how this resulted in *temporary* inconvenience—but that outcome was, on the whole, positive.

- A time when your own hard work and commitment caused minor resentment among peers. Talk about turning lemons into lemonade! The idea here is to talk about a "problem" rooted in the way your superior work ethic affects others. Point out how the difficulty was overcome, and make it clear that you go out of your way to develop relationships with others that are not intimidating in nature.

Here's an example of an "on-the-firing-line" response:

"The toughest challenge I've ever faced professionally? I guess that would have to be when I had to announce a round of layoffs. It was my job, so I didn't try to duck it, but I have to admit it was an experience that really tested my poise. I had to meet with each of the 15 people affected and pass along the news privately. Some of the people reacted maturely to the news, some didn't. There was one fellow who actually threatened me, but I was able to keep the situation from getting out of hand by reminding him that the layoffs had nothing to do with the quality of his work, but were simply an unavoidable response to the economic realities the firm was facing. That was probably the longest day of my life, getting through those meetings, but I did it."

"Tell me about the kinds of people you have to work to get along with."

With this question (another one likely to be delivered in a disarmingly informal way), the interviewer is asking you to seal your doom by revealing the various types of people you "can't stand." In answering it, remember that the categories of humanity you may feel tempted to unload on may be represented in significant numbers among your potential colleagues at the target organization!

No matter who gets on your nerves in real life, the best strategy to pursue in responding to this question is to pause, as though momentarily confused, before you even attempt to answer. People you don't get along with? What an interesting idea! Ponder this intriguing new possibility closely for a moment; give it the detached, professional review any new intellectual challenge deserves; and then say something along the following lines:

"Well, that's a tough one. I suppose that, like most people, I have trouble adjusting to people whose work ethic sometimes leaves a little bit to be desired. There was one time when I noticed a colleague slacking in a particularly obvious way when the boss was on vacation, and we exchanged a few heated words—in private—about what kind of example that set for some of the employees we had to supervise. But I look on that sort of exchange as a bump in the road. She and I never had any other notable problems interacting with one another that I can recall."

Ready, set...

If you've followed all the steps laid out in this chapter (and the other parts of the book to which you've been referred), you are now prepared to head off to the job interview and dazzle your prospective employer...provided that you take a look at the important preinterview checklist that appears in Chapter 8!

Chapter 6

If you have an interview in 8 to 14 days

You say you've got more than a week to get ready for an interview? That's great news! If you play your cards right, you should be in a perfect position to outshine your competitors for this job.

In fact, your greatest enemy here may well be *too much* time. That may sound absurd at first, but hear me out: In settings where you must—repeat *must*—make the most of your time before a professional interview, your attentions are likely to be more focused. (Remember the old Daffy Duck joke about how there's nothing like having a gun held to your head to concentrate your thinking? Preparing for an interview on short notice has a similar effect on one's focus.)

With more than a week to go before you sit down for a face-to-face meeting with your interviewer, you may find yourself procrastinating. "I'll nibble away at this a little at a time," you may think. "I've got enough lead time to get ready." Then *wham!* You check the calendar and realize your interview is right around the corner.

Don't wait until the last minute. Remember that getting a job *is* a full-time job, one that demands the same persistence and commitment of any other job worth having. Follow the advice that appears in this chapter as closely as you can, and do your best to put full attention and energy back on your research and preparation work *now*...so you can truly shine at the interview *later.*

Your first stop? The library, of course!

Let's assume that you've already developed the success stories we discussed in Chapter 1. Your primary destination is the biggest library you can stake out desk space at. If, for some reason, you *haven't* taken a close look at your own personal background and developed success stories highlighting your flexibility, your market orientation and your ability to look at things from a bottom-line perspective, you should do that now.

You're lucky enough to be able to spend at least three full, uninterrupted days at the library. (Yes, weekends count.) Budget your time sensibly and follow this advice:

Match your skills to the job description. Bring along a pen or pencil, plenty of paper and enough change to run the photocopier as much as you need to. You should also have a copy of the formal or informal job description we discussed in Chapter 3, because your first step will be to jot down as many matches as possible between your own accomplishments and the requirements of the job.

Mark all the parallels you can in your notebook. You will be on the lookout for opportunities to cite these connections during your interview.

You should spend at least a couple of hours developing *written* connections between your past work history and the job requirements you've unearthed. Writing this material down will help you remember it and refine your ideas.

Because you have a (comparatively) long span of time at your disposal, you have the luxury of developing several drafts of a document that outlines the various points of contact between what you offer and what the prospective employer is after. By the time you're done, you should be comfortable summarizing these points *in detail* at a moment's notice.

Search for articles and other information about the company. The more time you have, the more effort you can put into your search. It won't hurt to check the library's online databases (if these are available) or the *Reader's Guide to Periodical Literature* for listings that feature your target company's name. One of the advantage of a computerized search, of course, is that it allows you to scan the *entire text* of all the articles you've selected for any reference to the key word you've punched in.

Before too long, you should be able to get a good idea of how likely you are to find a direct reference to your employer in the mainstream press. If an hour or two of searching through the library's resources yields nothing, move on to the next step:

Check for the company's annual report. If you are applying to a public company, you will definitely want to track down a copy of the organization's annual report. This document features important information you must review closely before your interview. It should include mission statements, breakdowns of the organization's various business segments and, often, hints about future plans. It's all worth photocopying!

Because you have a little bit of time before your interview, you should make a point of tracking this report down, even if the various libraries in your area don't have a copy. Check at local educational institutions—business schools are a particularly good bet—or call the company's shareholder services line. A few intrepid job seekers have gone so far as to purchase a single share of stock in the company in order to obtain a copy of the annual report!

Check for books about or related to your target company. Once your efforts to track down a copy of the annual report have concluded, you should make a *quick* check of the library's main card catalog for any books that seem likely to be of interest, either because they deal directly with the target company or because they shed new light on the industry within which you'll be interviewing.

Don't attempt to read the books you find from cover to cover—scan their tables of contents and make a brief note of the passages that seem likely to be worth reviewing later.

Read trade magazines. You should review the last 15 to 20 issues of any appropriate industry publication. The idea is not to read every word of these vitally important "insider" publications, but to review them all *briefly* for key articles. Which new technologies are likely to affect the way your target company does business? What competitor is launching a new product or service? What is the biggest challenge the president of your target company is likely to face over the next 12 months?

Note all the answers on your pad, or make photocopies of appropriate articles for later study.

Develop a profile of the organization's typical customer. Whether that customer is an institution or an individual consumer punching an 800 number into a telephone—or a combination of the two—you should have an idea of who the target company sells its products or services to. Pay attention to the types of advertisements the company places and to *where* it places these advertisements. If you feel you've hit a dead end in your research, appeal to the librarian for help.

Do some brainstorming

The research you've conducted up to this point should give you a pretty good idea of the type of company you'll be meeting with. Now ask yourself: If you were in charge of coming up with the next revenue-generating or efficiency-enhancing idea for this company, what would you propose?

Yes, this amounts to doing a little bit of free work for your target employer. Rather than obsessing about whether you'll be properly compensated for your troubles, commit to go the extra mile. Spend some time developing a concept you can *briefly but confidently* appeal to during the interview. For example, take a look at something that one of the company's major competitors is doing, but that your target company is not, and ask about the possibility of doing something along those lines.

How many job applicants walk in the door with a profitable idea that's ready to use or adapt? Not many. By going the extra mile in this way, you will very likely set yourself apart from your competitors in a striking and distinctive way.

Work up an employment portfolio

What is an employment portfolio? It's a big book—preferably one with massive, snazzy black covers and some means of securing and removing documents easily. Your employment portfolio should be a *visual* embodiment of the strong points of your candidacy, and it should include these elements:

- Several copies of a *specifically targeted* resume, one designed with this position in mind. This is one great place to show off all those connections between your skills and what the employer is after. (In an ideal world, this should be the resume you submit for the position in the first place, but let's face it, this world of ours is not always ideal.)

- Copies of stellar written endorsements.

- Copies of college diplomas, certificates or any other documents worth including. (Don't bother with high-school diplomas, though.)

- Striking newsletters, articles or designs for which you were partly or fully responsible.

- Awards or honors for work-related achievements.

- Anything else that supports your candidacy with a strong visual message.

If you've got the time to work out the layout ahead of time—and if you can execute flawlessly, without typographical or layout errors—an employment portfolio can add a big boost to your application. It can add structure to your interview (a big help for clueless managers who don't know what to ask about next), and will almost certainly make you more memorable than the competition.

Map this portfolio out with any time you have left after completing all your other library work; execute it with impeccable neatness once you've prepared for all the interview questions discussed on pages 89 through 95. (Enlist the aid of a friend, too. A document is not proofread unless you *and someone else you trust* has read and signed off on it.)

Portfolios are not just for people in the graphic arts. They add a visual element to your presentation and will, if nothing else, help keep you from blending into the rest of the crowd. In assessing the various candidates afterwards, the interviewer may think, "Well, there's the fellow from that Ivy League university, the woman who won the Nobel Peace Prize...and that intriguing person who brought in that big black portfolio with all the endorsements. Hmm..."

Once you've outlined what should go into your employment portfolio, you should take time to assemble and proofread it if, and only if, you have thoroughly reviewed your library research and completed preparing for all of the interview questions outlined in the later sections of this chapter.

Prepare for commonly asked questions

Before you start preparing your answers to the interview questions covered in this chapter, you should devote your time to working up responses to the more common queries covered in Chapters 3, 4 and 5:

- "Tell me about yourself."
- "Why are you considering leaving your current position?"
- "Why did you leave your previous position?"
- "Wouldn't you have difficulty adapting to the way we do things around here?"
- "What's your greatest strength?"
- "What's your greatest weakness?"
- "What do you see yourself doing five years from now?"
- "Do you have any questions before we conclude?"
- "How has your job search been going?"
- "What don't you like about your current boss?"
- "Why should we hire you?"
- "What strengths and weaknesses did your supervisor identify for you on your most recent performance review?"
- "Why should we assume you'll stick around for a while if we hire you?"
- "What's your management philosophy?"
- "What salary level are you seeking?"
- "How do you approach the job of making key decisions?"
- "What do you want from your next job?"
- "How do you approach personal time management?"
- "What's the most challenging situation you've ever faced?"

- "Tell me about the kinds of people you have to work to get along with."

These are essential questions that you *must* be ready to handle before you walk into the interview. Set aside appropriate amounts of time to develop responses to each that reflect your own background and career strengths. Please remember as you do so that your answers must not sound canned. Practice answers to every one of the questions above *out loud*. Then proceed to the interview questions that follow and do the same for them.

"What would you say if I told you that your interview here today was the worst I'd ever witnessed?"

There are only two situations where you are likely to hear a question like this. In the first situation, you will be dealing with a shrewd manager who wants to see exactly how you deal with stress or conflict, probably because the job you're interviewing for is stressful.

In the second situation, you will have simply hooked up with a monumental jerk. In either case, you must project supreme unflappability if you hope to keep your options open. (Hey, you may actually decide, for whatever reasons, that you do want to work on a day-to-day basis with a jerk.)

When dealing with this or any other absurdly combative question, bear in mind that the worst thing that can happen during an interview is not intimidation, but obliviousness. The interviewer obviously has enough interest in you to have *posed* this antagonistic query, rather than smiling, shaking your hand and seeing you out the door.

If you encounter this question (or any stress question), delivered in a way that seems calculated to throw you for a loop, remember that you are always free to perform a silent translation before responding. Pretend that the interviewer has really asked you something along the lines of, "What would you do if someone said something this outrageous to you in a work setting? Would you react out of anger and polarize the situation further, or would you check for facts to learn more about the situation you faced?" Once you've considered the "attack" in this way, you'll be ready to respond along the following lines:

"Well, I guess I'd ask you if there had been any particular element of my presentation here today that had caused you to have doubts about my interviewing skills. Then I'd check whatever aspect of the interview you highlighted to make sure that I had sent the message I really intended to send. If I found that there was a communication problem somewhere along the line, I'd try to find some better way to phrase the idea I was trying to get across, and I'd give it another try."

"Who's one of your heroes?"

This question, which is designed to find out how you think on your feet and what kinds of values guide you, has many sneaky variations. One common one is this: "Tell me about the last book you read." Beware of trying to fake your way through a discussion of a book you haven't really read! Another twist sounds like this: "Who do you think the most important person in history was?"

These questions are *not* excuses to exchange snatches of *Brady Bunch* trivia with the interviewer, even if Greg really was one of the most important role models of your childhood! The interviewer is giving you the opportunity to hold forth on something of importance to you.

But you must bear in mind that the objective is not to establish a friendly social dialogue, but to send signals that portray you as responsible, thorough, open to new ideas, mindful of the value of old ones and utterly accountable for your actions. In short, to present yourself as the perfect applicant. In other words, it's better to choose an answer that portrays your positive traits than it is to offer one that offers an up-to-the-minute reflection of your aesthetic and literary inclinations.

A job interview is *always* about determining whether you're the right person for the job, even when it *sounds* like it might be about something else.

Warning! Some interviewers may choose an innocent-sounding question like this one to launch a sudden assault on you during the follow-up. These interviewers may, for instance, ask if you've read a particular book: "Have you read Janet Malcolm's *The Silent Woman?*" If you haven't read the book and if you have a healthy skepticism for faking your way through discussions about books you haven't read, you are well-advised to answer no.

But the interviewer may pick that moment to turn up the pressure! "What do you *mean,* you've never read *The Silent Woman?* It's the single most important book about the Plath phenomenon to come out in the last five years! Your own resume says that this woman was the topic of your senior thesis! Even if the book came out after you completed your work on that project, you can't expect me to believe you let this one slip past you. Don't tell me you didn't pick this book up after the reviews it got!"

Social and conversational instinct may tempt you to amend your initial answer and maintain that you *did* read all or part of the book in question, or at least see an excerpt somewhere. That's just what the interviewer wants you to do. What's at issue here is not your familiarity with *The Silent Woman,* but your ability to stand your ground.

The interviewer wants to know, "Is this one the kind to massage facts into whatever shape a superior requires, or is he or she more likely to report events accurately, even when under pressure?"

Even if things get strange, *do not reverse course.* Find a way to inform the interviewer politely that you knew what you were talking about when the question was first posed, and that nothing has changed since then. Hey, nobody said it was going to be *fun* to deal with stress questions.

Here's an example of one way to respond:

"Oh, there are a lot of people I look up to in history, but if I had to pick one, I suppose it would have to be Harry Truman. I just finished David McCullough's biography, which was marvelous and very inspiring. I think Truman proved what's possible if you stick to your guns, work hard and don't try to be anyone other than who you are.

"I was particularly impressed with the incident early in his career in which he refused to pass along public- works contracts that would benefit the political machine that had elected him, because he knew the quality of the vendors involved wasn't up to snuff. He knew what his job was, and he didn't deviate from it. Truman was a real inspiration; he's the person I'd pick as a role model if I had to choose one from 20th- century history."

However you choose to answer this question, you are best advised to pick *noncontroversial* people, publications and events—and to steer clear of religion! No matter what your assessment of the interviewer's tastes and/or political leanings, you probably don't want to get into a point-by- point analysis of on any topic that's likely to alienate a good chunk of the population. Even if you feel strongly in either direction about a topic such as the death penalty, abortion or gun control, you are better off choosing a book or person that your interviewer will be able to embrace as easily as you do.

"Do you mind if I contact your references?"

A good many employers will also ask permission to talk to your present employer, too, although *why* they think this is an appropriate course of action is certainly an open question. "No, of course not. My present employer, who is under the impression that I'm sick today, will probably be very interested to learn that I'm interviewing for a job elsewhere. If you call my supervisor, it will certainly keep things from getting boring around the office. Let's give it a try and see what happens."

Your best course is to point such employers toward a direct conversation with one of your references, and to stall for time while you alert the person who is recommending you to expect a call from Ms. So-and-so of ABC Company.

> *"I'd be more than happy to set up a call with my old supervisor back at the company I used to work for, DEF Industries. Why don't we handle it this way: I'll go through my files and track down his current number as soon as I get home. I'll leave word on your voice-mail machine if I can't reach you directly, probably no later than tomorrow afternoon."*

"What do you like to do when you're not working?"

Finally! A chance for you to relax and tell your interviewer all about the things you really like to do in your spare time, right? Wrong.

You are still on the spot. Before you confess your propensity to spend hours on end in front of a computer screen playing Alien Invasion 4.0, or your habit of whiling away whole weekends attending to your thimble collection, consider this: Many employers ask this question for the express purpose of determining whether you are a solitary type—as opposed to the kind of person who prefers to interact with others during your leisure time. As a very general rule, better job offers and salary packages go to those in the latter category.

So you were *really* about to hold forth on how much you enjoy your weekly bowling league or a good game of Trivial Pursuit, right? I thought so.

Just as you would when addressing the question of books you've read or people you admire, keep your answer *noncontroversial.* If you spend all or most of your time advocating a particular social cause, highlighting that may make you come of as a bit of a zealot, no matter how pure your intentions. *Don't focus on that part of your life in answering this question.* Your aim is to get hired, not to convince your interviewer of the worthiness of your cause.

The messages to get across here are pretty straightforward: You're not an idealogue. You don't spend most of your time on your own. You enjoy learning new things from other people.

> *"Oh, let's see. There's a sewing group I get together with every Friday night; we call ourselves the Ladies of the Order of Sip and Sew. I've learned a lot about cross-stitch technique from that group—I think I'm the youngest member of the bunch—but the truth is there's about as much talking during any given half-hour period as there is stitching.*

> *"This group offers us the chance to keep up with any television programs we may have missed, talk about what's happening in each person's family and maybe, if we're feeling particularly inspired, share some insights on how to handle a particularly challenging needlework pattern.*

> *"One of the pieces I finished ended up winning second place at the Topsfield Fair last year! I was pretty proud of that, but I don't think I could have pulled it off without having had my friends there showing me how to execute some of the trickier stitches."*

Ready to move on?

If you've followed all the advice in this chapter and intelligently budgeted your available time to the tasks described, your main job now is to *take good care of yourself.* You will want to look and sound your best for the interview, and that means getting enough sleep, getting enough to eat, attending to your personal hygiene, and picking out the right outfit. See Chapter 8 for a full listing of the points you should attend to before heading out the door.

All the research and answer preparation in the world won't help you if you follow the fashion and grooming example of a computer programmer I once had to interview. He showed up for our meeting smelling as though he hadn't bathed in a week, sporting two and a half days' worth of beard growth and wearing a T-shirt and jeans! As if that weren't enough, the jeans were...not snug. They hung down halfway to his hips, affording me a privileged view of his underwear.

If this was a conscious fashion statement, I concluded, it wasn't the right one to make during a professional interview. If it was simply an oversight, it was the kind that made me wonder what kind of impression this person would be likely to make when interacting with fellow employees...or representing the company to outsiders!

Chapter 7

If you have an interview in more than 14 days

You've got more than two weeks to prepare before your interview is to take place? That's wonderful news. Just be sure not to procrastinate when it comes to finding out all you can about your target company.

In situations where you have a comparatively long timeline to prepare for your interview, it is probably even more important to set aside library research time *early* in the preparation process. Why? Because of the danger that you will put the task of researching your prospective employer until the very last minute!

You must take advantage of the time at your disposal, budget your days carefully and take full advantage of any weekend or personal days you can squeeze into the job of preparing for your interview.

Head to the biggest, best-supplied library you can find—*right now*, not next week. Be ready to commit to at least three to four days of uninterrupted research between now and the day of your interview, and schedule those days as early as possible. By taking full advantage of the time at your disposal to find out everything you possibly can about the target company, you will give yourself a virtually unbeatable advantage when it comes to scoring points with the prospective employer.

Your action plan at the library

Assuming that you've taken the time to develop your personal success stories, as outlined in Chapter 1, your first job will be to take a good, long look at the (formal or informal) job description of the position for which you will be competing. As outlined elsewhere in this book, you *must* find some way to isolate the requirements of this position as the prospective employer defines them. Usually, it's not very difficult to track these requirements down. See Chapter 3 for some ideas.

Because you've got a good deal of time at your disposal, you should plan on spending a full day developing points of contact between your own background and experiences and the requirements of the job.

Write these parallels down in a notebook (doing so will help you reinforce and memorize key points); develop *several drafts* of this "closing argument." You should be prepared to appeal to these connections at any point during your interview, but you will, in all likelihood, find that it's most effective to make your appeal to the "fit" you've discovered near the end of your meeting.

Check for articles about the target company. Review the library's collection of mainstream magazines for articles that refer to your target company directly. This will be considerably easier to do if the library you've selected features an online key word search or article retrieval system. If it doesn't, take a look at the appropriate volume of the *Reader's Guide to Periodical Literature.* Some companies, of course, won't be the subject of any articles in the mainstream press. If this is the case for your target company, proceed to the next step of your library research.

Look for an annual report. If the company is publicly held, you should track down a copy of the firm's annual report and read it thoroughly. If the library doesn't have one and/or can't point you toward one, consider contacting the company's office of shareholder services.

The annual report will clue you in on all sorts of important information about the organization's mission statement, business segments and long-term goals. Make appropriate note of all relevant facts and photocopy any portions of the annual report that seem worthy of later review.

If the document incorporates a mission statement or message from the president or CEO, you may want to consider memorizing a brief passage for recitation at an appropriate point of the interview. It may sound silly at first, but the act of reciting an important passage from this can make a remarkable impression on an interviewer.

Before you move on to the next step, make a quick check of the library's main catalog for any books that directly reference your target company or the industry within which it operates. Scan these volumes for key facts, but don't waste a whole research day on a book that only has a marginal connection to your target employer.

Head for the trade magazines. These are the journals of immediate and pressing interest to key decisionmakers within your industry. Ask the librarian for help if you are not sure which magazines or journals you should be looking for.

Most of the people you'll be competing with won't take the time and trouble to review these publications. You, however, will—and you'll be far more likely to leave a good impression with the interviewer as a result! Devote a full day to the task of reviewing as many of these essential "industry insider" publications as you can. Don't attempt to read them line-for-line and cover-to-cover, but do keep an eye out for articles that seem to directly relate to the challenges and opportunities key people at your target organization would face.

Ask yourself: Who's the customer? One of the big advantages of having more time on your hands to research the target company is that you've got the opportunity to use all the resources of your library to identify the organization's typical customers. If you need to, you should enlist the help of a reference librarian in this task.

Who buys what this company offers? The answer may be a few huge corporations, a single government agency, a group of retailers or tens of thousands of consumers from a particular demographic group who buy direct from the firm via telephone or catalog. Whatever the answer, you should be familiar with it before you walk in the door for your interview.

Come up with a great idea. You should also leave aside some time during your stay at the library to develop a new idea of potential benefit to the organization you will be interviewing with. This idea could take the form of a new product, a variation on an old one, a reaction to a move by a competitor, a new and more efficient way of doing things— anything, really, that is likely to make your interviewer sit up, take notice and think, "Hey, this person might actually make life a little easier around here."

Set aside a specific period of time to use the library's resources in the development of your idea. During your interview, keep an ear open for an opportunity to make *tactful* reference to your suggestion. Focus on initiatives that will complement the organization's current activities.

Be careful that you don't come off as arrogant or overbearing. You won't, of course, say something like this: "You know what you people need to do?" Or "I can't believe you've overlooked this..." or anything that implies the company is making inept decisions.

Prepare your employment portfolio. It's important to develop a sharp-looking, colorful, carefully proofread and neatly assembled portfolio that highlights your special skills, achievements, ideas and interests—and also sneaks in a visual component to your candidacy for the interviewer's benefit.

This visual element is an advantage you should not overlook, especially if your interview happens to fall during one of the "dead slots" that may reduce the likelihood of the interviewer remembering you at all. (If *you* were interviewing 16 people over three days, and were talking to number 15 right before lunch on a day when you'd skipped breakfast, you'd probably need a little help recalling names and credentials, too.)

You'll probably want to work up an outline at the library, then execute the portfolio at home. Make sure it includes a targeted copy of your resume (and bring an extra copy of the resume for your interviewer, too). Track down an impressive-looking black binder and go through the high points at an appropriate point in the interview. Your interviewer may appreciate your advance work, because it will save him or her the trouble of having to structure a sequence of questions if he or she hasn't done so! The two of you may end up simply working your way through the portfolio page by page, with the interviewer posing appropriate queries.

Interview for practice

"What else should I do if I've got a little extra time on my hands?" If you feel comfortable with the most important questions the interviewer is likely to toss your way, one of the best things you can do to prepare for an important interview is to *interview somewhere else for practice!* This may mean sitting down with a company representative to discuss a job that you *(ssh!)* wouldn't really be interested in. Or it may mean that you corral a friend or relative for a little role-playing.

Rehearse your answers to the most commonly asked questions

Before you start working on responses to the interview questions covered in detail later in this chapter, you should devote some time to coming up with customized answers to the queries covered in Chapters 3 through 6:

- "Tell me about yourself."

- "Why are you considering leaving your current position?"

- "Why did you leave your previous position?"

- "Would you have difficulty adapting to the way we do things around here?"

- "What's your greatest strength?"

- "What's your greatest weakness?"

- "What do you see yourself doing five years from now?"

- "Do you have any questions before we conclude?"

- "How has your job search been going?"

- "What don't you like about your current boss?" or, "What did you like least about your old boss?"

- "Why should we hire you?"

- "What strengths and weaknesses did your supervisor identify for you on your most recent performance review?"

- "Why should we assume you'll stick around if we hire you?"

- "What's your management philosophy?"

- "What salary level are you seeking?"

- "How do you approach the job of making key decisions?"

- "What do you want from your next job?"

- "How do you approach personal time management?"

- "What's the most challenging situation you've ever faced?"

- "Tell me about the kinds of people you have to work to get along with."

- "Who's one of your heroes?"

- "What's your favorite book?"

- "What would you say if I told you your interview was among the most incompetent I'd ever witnessed?"

- "Do you mind if I contact your references?"

- "What kinds of things do you do when you're not working?"

Budget your time in such a way as to allow yourself appropriate amounts of time to develop your own unique responses to each, responses that don't sound "canned" and that reflect your own skills and accomplishments.

Rehearse your answers to every one of the questions referenced above *out loud*. Then move on to the interview questions that appear here and do the same for them, following the advice laid out after each.

"What would you do if your boss left you in charge of a vitally important project and couldn't be reached once you realized there was a serious problem he or she hadn't anticipated?"

This type of question is known as a "situational" interview query. This particular inquiry is probably meant to determine how you handle a crisis as well as how comfortable you are with making decisions. Your aim in responding to it should be to demonstrate your respect for systems, procedures and hierarchies *and* demonstrate that you're quite capable of showing the necessary personal initiative.

Your answer might sound like this:

"Well, my first step would be to exhaust all the reasonable ways I could come up with for getting in touch with my boss. I would leave messages on voicemail, e-mail and a home phone as well. If I couldn't get in touch with him (or her) that day, I'd go to my supervisor's boss and ask for input. But first, I'd come up with some solutions on my own that I thought my supervisor would approve of and recommend these."

"How would you approach the aspects of this job that aren't particularly exciting?"

This one's likely to come your way after you've gone into some rhapsody about how interesting you find the prospect of working within your chosen industry. The prospective employer is hoping to alert you to the fact that some of the tasks associated with the job are routine, and perhaps even a little boring.

Show the interviewer that you fully understand what you're getting into and are eager to pursue the opportunity nonetheless. You may wish to conclude by adapting one of your success stories to illustrate your point. The answer here incorporates a success story that highlights your bottom-line awareness.

"I realize that every job has its routine elements, and I certainly realize that this one, an entry-level position, probably has more than some others. But this is the job I want, and it's one I feel I could make an important contribution to.

"It's nice to be able to focus on new, creative solutions, and when called upon to do that I'd certainly be eager to make a contribution. But repetitious tasks have to be done, too, and they have to be done well.

"I'd consider fulfilling that goal one of my strong suits, actually—I have a real passion for detail. Once, in my current position, my supervisor asked us to take two days to double-check his inventory figures, because he had some suspicions that some of the counts were off. A few of my colleagues were less than thrilled with the prospect, but I saw it as a chance to save the company money, and sure enough, that's what I ended up doing. I found a $4,000 error!"

"How would you learn what you needed to know in order to perform at a high level in this job?"

This question should leap out at you as an opportunity to show off one of the success stories you developed to highlight your flexibility and adaptability.

These days, many employers are looking for people who are willing to take a little initiative to track down the knowledge they need. Tell the interviewer about some aspect of your own work experience that illustrates your ability to bring yourself up to speed on key issues.

"To tell you the truth, I don't think I'd have much difficulty getting myself up and running. Most of the people I've worked for have commented on the fact that I'm a pretty quick study.

"In my previous position, for instance, there was a deadline crunch, and the production department needed help developing computer-generated technical drawings. There was no time for training sessions—so I took the software manuals home and ran a few of the tutorials on my own machine.

"The next morning, I was parked in front of the production department's terminals, executing the drawings. The head of the department was pleased and said they looked quite strong. We made the 72-hour deadline, and the people in production used to joke that they were planning to steal me away from my supervisor!"

"What would you do if a customer called up complaining about a technological problem?"

The interviewer is out to test your claims of technical mastery in a particular area. Be sure you know your stuff. The specifics of your answer, of course, will depend on your own background and experience and the nature of the problem the interviewer tosses your way.

But there are two key points to keep in mind before you start outlining potential solutions. First, the interviewer will almost certainly be listening to whether you attempt to seek out more information and quantify the particulars of the situation. Don't assume that the question will present you with all the data you need.

Second, be forewarned that different organizations may employ different terminologies to describe the same materials or procedures. Make a point of explaining phrases that may be misunderstood—or not understood at all.

Here's an example of an answer to this potentially difficult question:

"Actually, I had a query from a customer who said that the screen display on his computer showed only horizontal lines after he installed a Veribrite graphics card. Can I assume that we'd be talking about a situation similar to that one?

"Well, I walked the customer through the process of reinstalling the card, step-by-step, over the telephone. I followed the steps outlined on my TRO—that's a term we use at my current employer for the written outlines of common solutions to customer problems—and it turned out that the problem was a command that had been improperly entered very early on in the process.

"It was understandable that the customer would have a problem here, because he had had to enter a 15-digit number from the manual. He'd simply transposed two of the numbers. That situation worked out well: The customer was pretty hot under the collar when he first contacted me, but by the end of the conversation he was saying how happy he was with the technical support our company offered."

"How familiar are you with our organization?"

Because you've faithfully carried out all the advice on up-front research that appears earlier in this chapter, you should have no problem with this type of question.

Most applicants don't take the trouble to do *any* meaningful research on the target company before they sit down for an interview. It probably shouldn't be too surprising, then, that a good many people are left to shift nervously in their seats and smile broadly after responding "Not that much, really," to this question.

Fortunately, that's not you. Here's an example of how you can make reference to some of the most important facts you've dug up during your library research phase.

"Oh, I've learned a lot of fascinating things about your company. As a matter of fact, that's the main reason I'm sitting here talking to you today. My research indicates that your firm and I could accomplish some great things together.

"For one thing, I learned from your annual report that you're hoping to expand into the library market within the next 18 months. As it happens, I spent a great deal of time in my last position developing some innovative new approaches for marketing directly to public and private library systems.

"I also found out from an article in Publishers Weekly *that you were among the first publishers to develop a solid presence on the Internet as a marketing and promotional tool. I've made several visits to your web site, and I found it absolutely fascinating. If we have time a little later on, we may be able to talk about some related web sites that you could hook that site up to that would increase the number of hits you get from retailers and librarians.*

"I also tracked down a copy of an interview Minneapolis Monthly *conducted with the president of your organization. He mentioned that developing new, nonretail marketing channels was one of his highest priorities, and I'd like to think I'm one of the people who's going to be able to help him attain that goal."*

Now what?

If you've followed all the advice in this chapter (and the other parts of the book referenced here), you're ready to make a great impression during your interview. But be sure to consult the next chapter for the last-minute checklist that will help you avoid some of the most common first-impression errors!

Chapter 8

Before you head out the door

You've done the research. You have prepared for the questions you're likely to face. You've even set up a snazzy-looking employment portfolio and come up with a great new idea for the target organization. What could go wrong?

Plenty, actually. Here's a list of questions you should ask yourself before you head for your interview. Don't skip any! (Some of these elements have already been covered in earlier passages, but these steps are so important that they're definitely worth repeating here.)

- *Have you gotten a good night's sleep?* All your preparation work will have been in vain if you show up exhausted and deliver a rambling, incoherent assessment of what you have to offer the company.

- *Have you groomed yourself carefully?* You'd be surprised how many applicants show up for an interview looking as though they'd failed Hygiene 101. Don't be one of them.

- *Is your interview attire appropriate?* Keep it simple. Keep it sharp. Keep it clean. Dress a little more formally than you would if you were an employee at the target organization. The navy-blue-suit look is your safest bet whether you're male or female. Don't go overboard on jewelry, cologne, perfume or other distractions.

Last Minute Interview Tips

- *Have you called ahead to confirm your directions?* Ideally, you should practice driving to the interview site beforehand, but sometimes this isn't possible. If you're traveling to an unfamiliar site, leave *plenty* of time to get lost. If you end up arriving early, kill a little time at a bookstore or coffee shop, but make sure you arrive for your interview at least five minutes before the scheduled time.

  If your interviewer asks whether you had any trouble finding the place, smile and say no, and don't get into a long discussion about who gave you directions or how early you arrived.

- *Have you brought an extra copy of your resume for the interviewer?* They lose things just like everyone else. Remember, your resume should be targeted to the specifics of the position you're interviewing for.

- *Have you remembered to be courteous and friendly to everyone you meet at the company—from the receptionist to your interviewer's assistant?* An important quality that every employer is looking for is the ability to work well with others. Make a positive impression on other employees. They may very well have some input in your interviewer's decision-making process.

- *Have you repeated the phrase "It's not brain surgery" to yourself silently several times?* It's not! Remember the sage advice of New York Yankees outfielder Mickey Rivers:

  > *"Ain't no use worrying about things you've got control over, because if you've got control over them, ain't no use worrying. Ain't no use worrying about things you don't have control over, because if you don't have control over them, ain't no use worrying."*

If there's a better piece of last-minute advice to pass on to someone who's a few minutes away from a meeting with a prospective employer, I haven't come across it.

You're cleared for takeoff!

Well, that's it. You're ready to start your adventure.

As you prepare for your encounter with the prospective employer, recall that a harmonious spirit and a sense of purpose are among your most important advantages. Recognize that there is potential benefit in virtually any situation, even one that seems a little intimidating at first.

The ancient Chinese book of wisdom, the *I Ching*, has this to say: "It will be advantageous to be firm and correct, and thus there will be free course and success. Let the reader nourish a docility like that of a cow, and there will be good fortune." Don't misunderstand this advice about "docility." The *I Ching* is not suggesting that we remain utterly passive in all our dealings with people. What the passage refers to is an inspired, discerning way of taking action, one that is purposeful, in complete harmony with others and ready to take instant advantage of so-called "coincidence." This mind-set is exactly the one you need when meeting with prospective employers—but it cannot be maintained in the face of fear!

Relax and enjoy the journey. You're about to make someone's day.

Appendix 1

Your post-interview follow-up campaign

Immediately after your interview—before you celebrate how well you think it went, agonize over how poorly you think it went or call your friends and relatives to update them on what happened—you should sit down someplace quiet and make extensive notes on as many details as you can remember about the interview.

Write down the names of any new people you interviewed with. Write down any new facts you unearthed about your target organization. Write down as many of the questions you were asked as you can remember. Write down what you think were the high and low points of the meeting. Write down *everything* in a notebook and date all your entries. You may need all this information later on down the line.

Now you can celebrate, agonize or call your friends and relatives. You've worked hard and deserve a break. Take it.

Before the day is out, though...

You must compose and send a personalized thank-you note. Send the note via regular mail on the day of your interview (or, if scheduling makes that impossible, first thing on the morning of the next day) *and* fax a copy to the person you met on the *next* day. In the event, your contact will receive the fax first, and the snail-mail a day or so later.

This shows off both thoroughness and a good sense of business etiquette.

Your personalized thank-you note should *briefly* emphasize whatever you feel to be the best part of the meeting you just concluded. Appeal to the notes you took immediately after the interview if you're not sure what part of the meeting that was.

Page 116 shows an example of what your note might look like. Note the tantalizing P.S.! This is often the part of the letter people read first.

"They said no!"

Hard to believe, I know, but it's possible that the prospective employer with whom you met won't offer you the job.

If you get a no, answer, you *must* avoid the temptation to fall into a fault-finding or blaming mode. Instead, you should smile in a genuine, undaunted way and react as though the answer were "not right now, thanks, but keep trying." Keep the lines of communication open with the prospective employer; ask in a nonthreatening way what caused the decision to go as it did; *politely* inform your contact that you'll be in touch again before too long to see if things have changed. Write down all the information you get in your notebook—the same one you used to jot down all the information about the interview immediately after it concluded. Review all that information closely; call back in 10 days or so and ask whether there's another opening you could interview for. During that phone call, highlight the aspects of your background that most impressed the interviewer the last time around.

When you receive word that you won't be getting a particular job offer, you haven't been issued the employment equivalent of a death sentence; to the contrary, you are now on this prospective employer's radar screen. Countless job seekers have taken a "no, thanks" from a prospective employer and turned it into a satisfying full-time position down the line. In this book's companion volume, *Last Minute Job Search Tips,* you'll find extensive advice on how to turn your rejection file into one of your most important job-search resources. Some tips include:

- If the interview results in a "no, but feel free to keep in touch" response, this is a good sign! Avoid the temptation to ask, "Well, *when?*" Instead, smile in a genuine, undaunted way and say, "You bet I will." And then call, say, a week and a half later.

- Count to 10, even if you feel frustrated when you get the news. A negative, overbearing or hostile reaction to a no outcome will only serve to convince your contact that rejecting you was the right decision. Following up on your rejections may constitute your *best statistical chance* to land a job. Every person you talk to within that organization should be accorded your best treatment. Every person you talk to within that organization— including administrative and support staff!—should be treated as a "live" employment lead.

- You live in a free country. You can call whoever you want, whenever you want, about the possibility of professional employment. Just be sure you come across as optimistic, professional, poised and nonthreatening in all your written and verbal contacts.

Keep at it. The people at your target company were interested enough in you to sit down and talk about a position. That means you may have a significant edge over the competition when the next opening materializes.

Jane Allen
654 Freedom Court
Cambridge MA 02138
617-555-1111

May 25, 1996

Frank Powell, Managing Editor
ABC Publishing
1 Tremont Street
Boston MA 02254

Dear Mr. Powell:

It was a real pleasure meeting with you to discuss
employment opportunities at ABC!

I was particularly excited about your company's efforts to
expand into the library market. I think my direct-mail
work at Hughes Associates, my current employer, could
be a real plus to you in that regard.

If there's anything else I can provide that will help you
evaluate my candidacy, I hope you will feel free to call
me at the number above.

Sincerely,

Jane Allen

Jane Allen

P.S. The "Rise and Shine" direct mail piece I left with
you, which I designed, resulted in $45,000 in revenues
over its first three months!

Appendix 2

Sample forms

Sample contact log form

Two sample forms you can adapt to your telephone contact work are on pages 118 and 119. Don't keep information for 20 of your prospective employers on the same sheet of paper. Photocopy the forms provided and you'll have enough room to take down all the information you need for each firm.

The *quicker* you want to get a job, the *more* prospective employers you should be contacting. Getting lulled into a false sense of security by a single "nibble" is what causes job searches to stall. Make copies of the form—then hit the library (to identify companies) and then the telephones! When in doubt, call the president and/or his or her assistant.

Sample targeted resume

In the resume on page 120, notice how the applicant has pointed the "career objective" portion of his resume directly toward the position for which he is applying *at this company*. If you don't want to revise your objective in this way, you should probably skip it altogether.

Nearly every aspect of this resume points directly or indirectly to writing, journalism or copy development skills. But the final paragraph, about volunteer work, highlights a significant, quantifiable increase in membership for which the applicant was responsible. Talk about bottom-line awareness!

Last Minute Interview Tips

Company Name:_____

Telephone:_____

Date of first call:_____

Contact:_____

Notes:_____

_____

Next step:_____

Second call:_____

Contact:_____

Notes:_____

_____

Next step:_____

Third call:_____

Contact:_____

Notes:_____

_____

Next step:_____

Fourth call:_____

Contact:_____

Notes:_____

_____

Next step:_____

Company's requirements for open position:

_____

_____

_____

Important: *Have you verified the spelling of the contact's name?*
Have you asked for a formal or informal job description for the job you want?
Has this company been sent a targeted resume and letter based on that job description?

Company Name:_____

Telephone:_____

Date of first call:_____

Contact:_____

Notes:_____

_____

Next step:_____

Second call:_____

Contact:_____

Notes:_____

_____

Next step:_____

Third call:_____

Contact:_____

Notes:_____

_____

Next step:_____

Fourth call:_____

Contact:_____

Notes:_____

_____

Next step:_____

Company's requirements for open position:

_____

_____

_____

Important: *Have you verified the spelling of the contact's name?*
Have you asked for a formal or informal job description for the job you want?
Has this company been sent a targeted resume and letter based on that job description?

AARON BENJAMIN
4175 Central Avenue
Brambleton, IL 60999
(312) 555-6775

Job Objective: Writer in Corporate Publications Department.

Education: Bachelor of Arts, Indiana University, 1994
Major: Journalism/Minor: Government
GPA: 3.5/4.0

Related Experience: *Indiana Daily Student* (student newspaper):
Features Editor, 1995-1996
Editorial Page Editor, 1994-1995
Staff Reporter, 1993-1994

Work Experience: *Brambleton Weekly Times:* Reporter, Business
Department, summers, 1991-1993
Wrote features on business owners and other
business-related news in Brambleton area;
edited copy of other writers. Trained new
interns in business department.

Honors/ Awards: Ernie Pyle Scholarship, Journalism Department,
1991 finalist, Sigma Delta Chi writing awards,
1992

Community Activities: **Member, Steering committee, Cancer
Awareness Campaign**
Responsible for disseminating information
(writing ad copy, public speaking) on health
issues to campus audiences.

**Vice President, Big Brothers campus
chapter**
Founded and developed first membership
drive for college Big Brother program;
increased chapter membership by 150% in
3 months.

Sample targeted cover letter

Here's a targeted cover letter that gets right to the point.

---

463 Hammerton Way   May 25, 1996
Cambridge, MA 02138

Ms. Ellen Sharp, V.P., Human Resources
Betterway Optical Equipment
656 Gerard Street
Boston, MA 02254

Dear Ms. Sharp:

After a brief discussion today with Becky, your receptionist, I think
I've identified some of the most important factors you're looking for
in a new sales manager:

- The ability to react quickly to sudden market shifts. (I
  guided the most successful launch of a new product in my
  company's history, the Presto-Scanner, and identified new
  corporate markets that accounted for 40,000 unit sales.)
- Strong familiarity with the optical industry. (I have
  attended the last four Optic World industry conferences as a
  representative of my current firm, and have followed your
  company's growth with great interest by keeping up with
  Optics Journal.)
- Ability to deliver bottom-line results. (Sales revenue in the
  department I currently manage has increased by at least 20%
  in each of the past four years.)

I'd like to talk to you about making a contribution to your firm as a
full-time employee. Enclosed please find my resume. I'll call you at
9:30 a.m. on Wednesday, April 3, to make sure these materials
reached you.

Sincerely,

Alan Bell

Alan Bell

P.S. If we can get together for an interview to discuss the current
opening, I guarantee that you will be glad you did so.

About the author

Brandon Toropov is a Boston-area writer who served as editor for a number of job-search bestsellers. His works include *303 Off-the-Wall Ways to Get a Job* and the companion volume to this book, *Last Minute Job Search Tips*.

His other books include the forthcoming *Who Was Eleanor Rigby?*, a book of Beatles trivia questions, and *The Everything Christmas Book*, on which he served as general editor.

Index

Last Minute Interview Tips